Gazzotti
Vehlmann

alone

8 The Arena

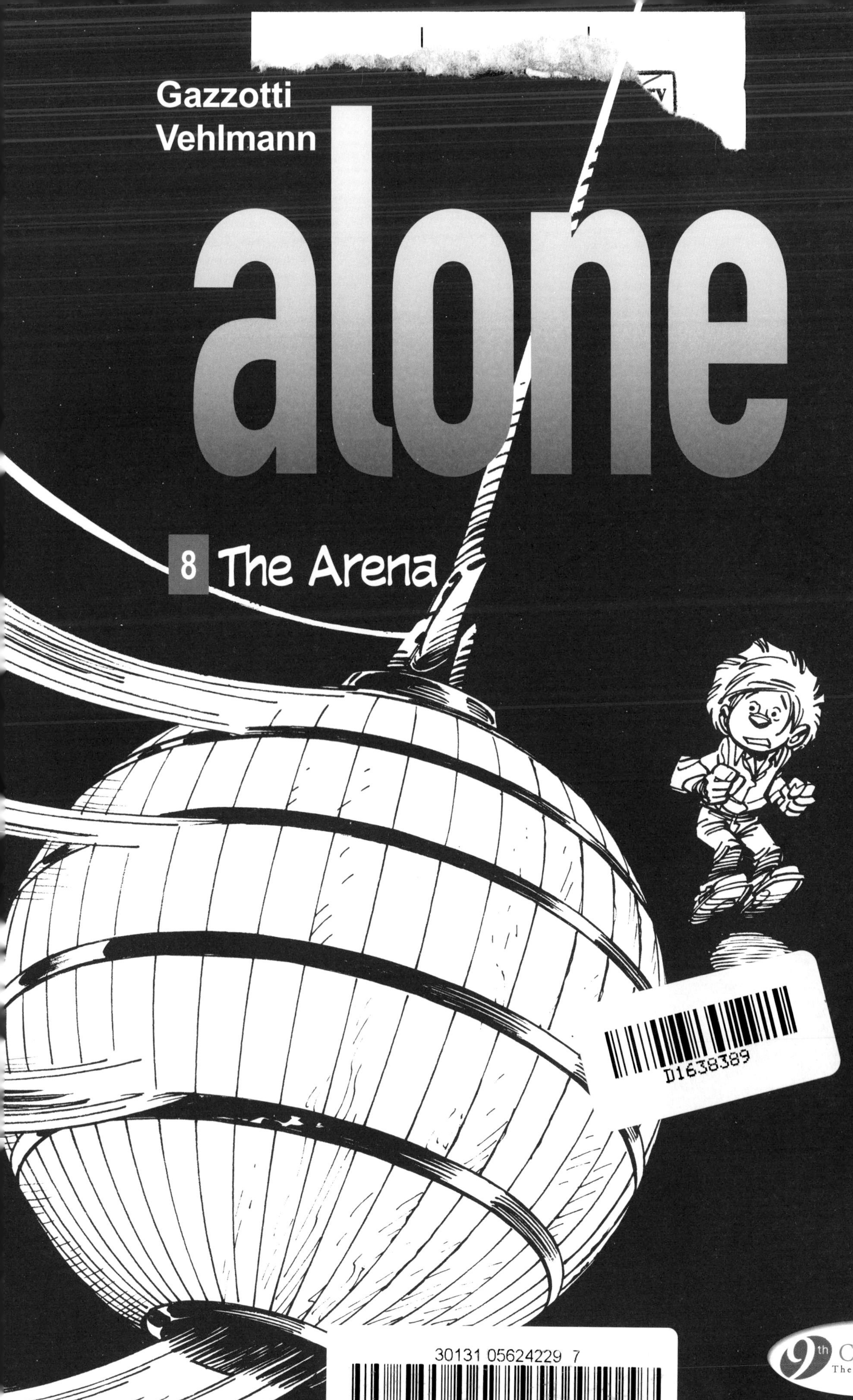

CINEBOOK
The 9th Art Publisher

First Autumn Song, by Charles Baudelaire
Translation by William Aggeler, *The Flowers of Evil* (Fresno, CA:
Academy Library Guild, 1954).

- To Nicolas Delhorme, in memory of a memorable meeting at the Lyon Festival.
Fabien
- My thanks to J.C., Lucie, Paty, Alain… and the André-Jacquemin family.
Bruno

Colours: Usagi

Original title: Seuls – Les Arènes
Original edition: © Dupuis, 2013 by Gazzotti & Vehlmann
www.dupuis.com
All rights reserved
English translation: © 2017 Cinebook Ltd
Translator: Jerome Saincantin
Editor: Erica Olson Jeffrey
Lettering and text layout: Design Amorandi
Printed in Spain by EGEDSA
This edition first published in Great Britain in 2018 by
Cinebook Ltd
56 Beech Avenue
Canterbury, Kent
CT4 7TA
www.cinebook.com
A CIP catalogue record for this book
is available from the British Library
ISBN 978-1-84918-382-6

9th CINEBOOK
The 9th Art Publisher

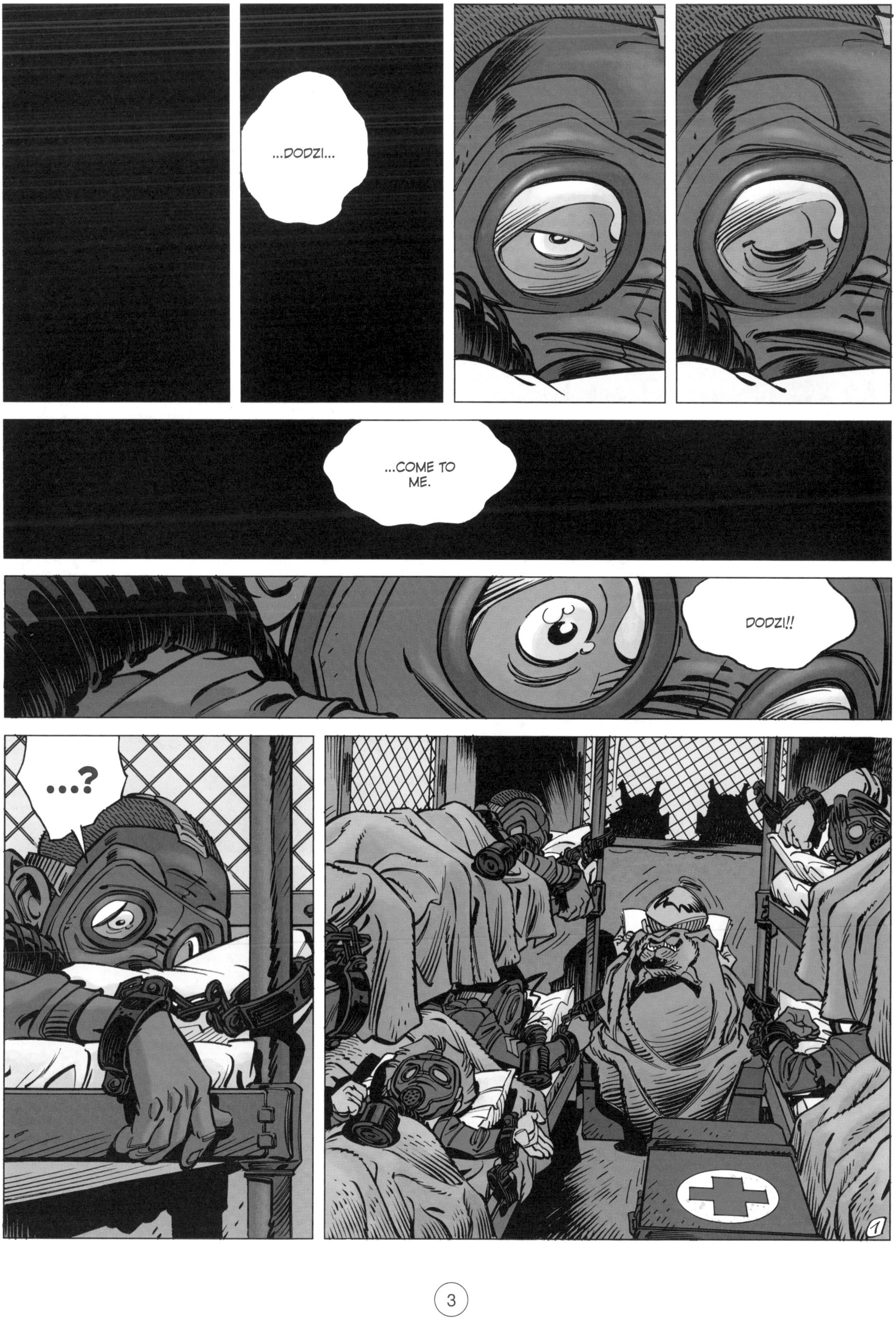
...DODZI...
...COME TO ME.
DODZI!!
...?

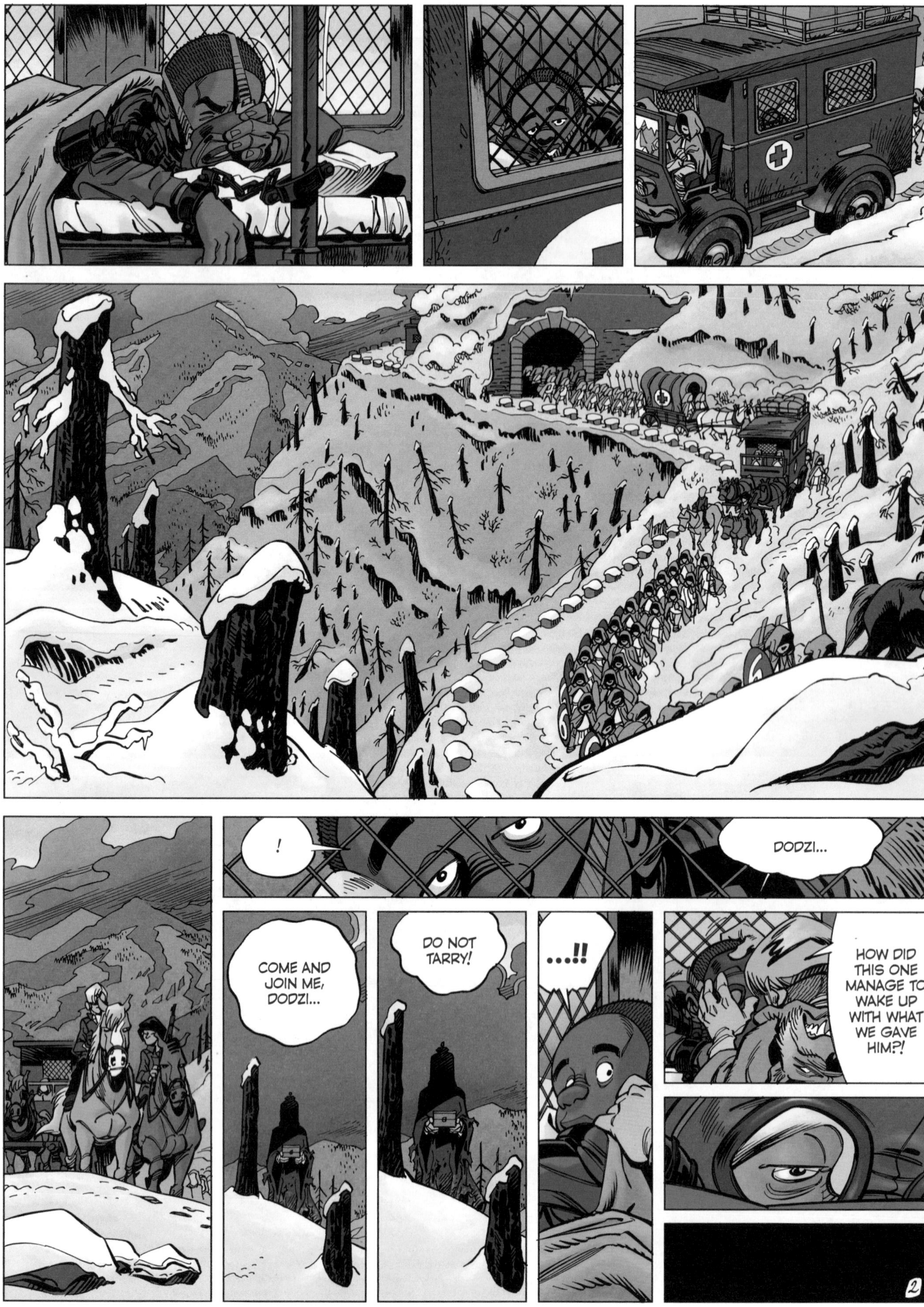
!
DODZI...
COME AND JOIN ME, DODZI...
DO NOT TARRY!
...!!
HOW DID THIS ONE MANAGE TO WAKE UP WITH WHAT WE GAVE HIM?!

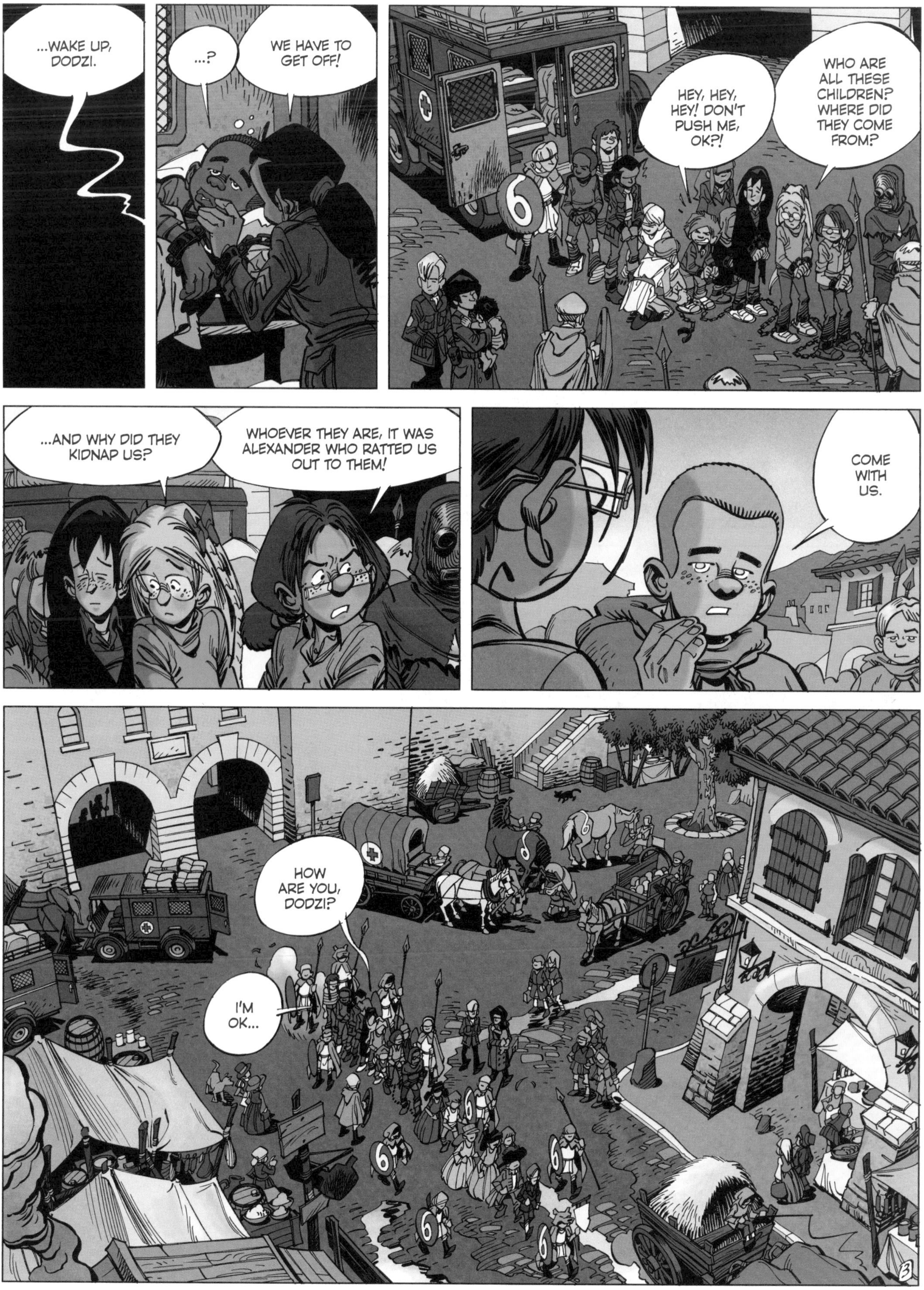
...WAKE UP, DODZI.
...?
WE HAVE TO GET OFF!
HEY, HEY, HEY! DON'T PUSH ME, OK?!
WHO ARE ALL THESE CHILDREN? WHERE DID THEY COME FROM?
...AND WHY DID THEY KIDNAP US?
WHOEVER THEY ARE, IT WAS ALEXANDER WHO RATTED US OUT TO THEM!
COME WITH US.
HOW ARE YOU, DODZI?
I'M OK...

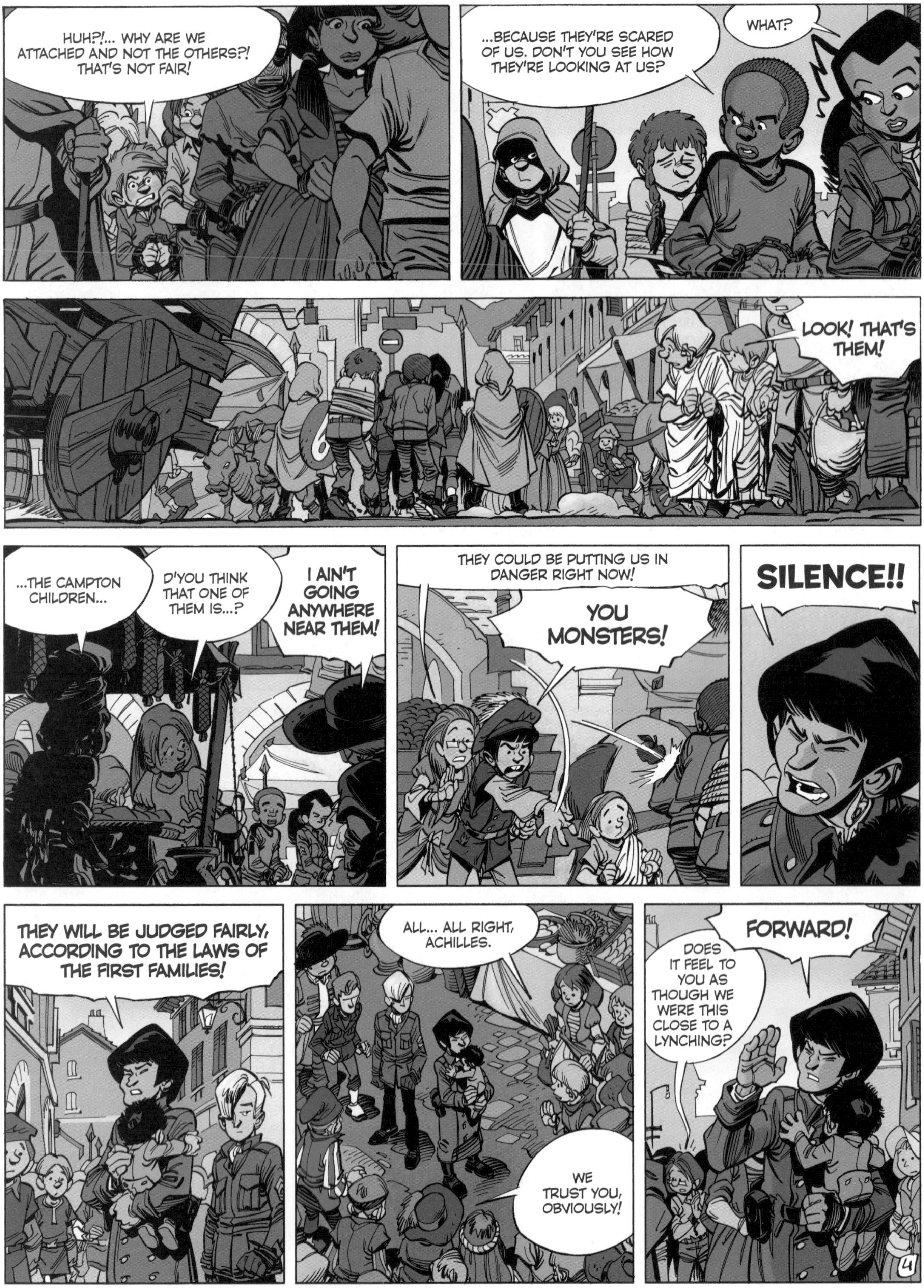
HUH?!... WHY ARE WE ATTACHED AND NOT THE OTHERS?! THAT'S NOT FAIR!
...BECAUSE THEY'RE SCARED OF US. DON'T YOU SEE HOW THEY'RE LOOKING AT US?
WHAT?
LOOK! THAT'S THEM!
...THE CAMPTON CHILDREN...
D'YOU THINK THAT ONE OF THEM IS...?
I AIN'T GOING ANYWHERE NEAR THEM!
THEY COULD BE PUTTING US IN DANGER RIGHT NOW!
YOU MONSTERS!
SILENCE!!
THEY WILL BE JUDGED FAIRLY, ACCORDING TO THE LAWS OF THE FIRST FAMILIES!
ALL... ALL RIGHT, ACHILLES.
WE TRUST YOU, OBVIOUSLY!
FORWARD!
DOES IT FEEL TO YOU AS THOUGH WE WERE THIS CLOSE TO A LYNCHING?

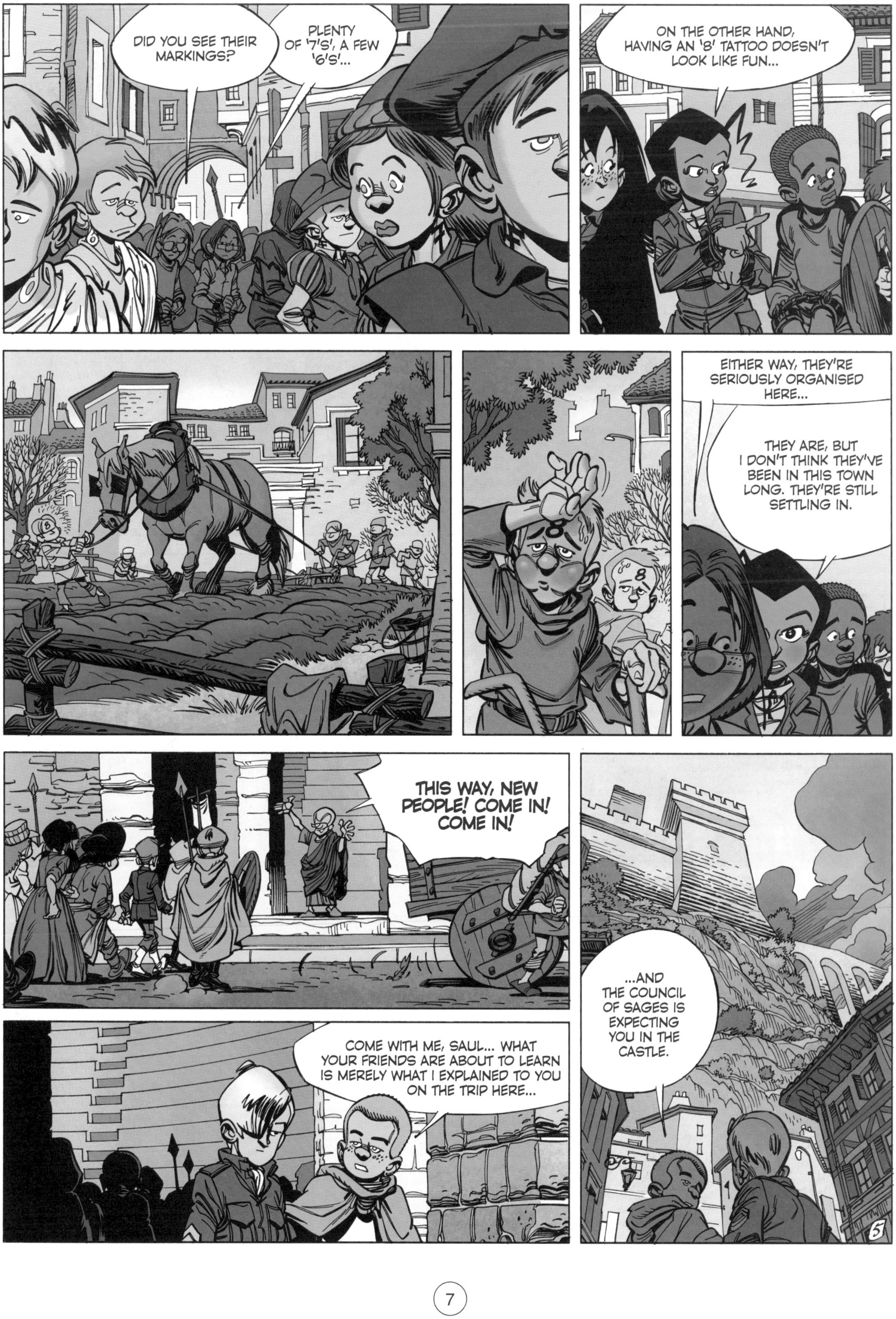
DID YOU SEE THEIR MARKINGS?
PLENTY OF '7'S', A FEW '6'S'...
ON THE OTHER HAND, HAVING AN '8' TATTOO DOESN'T LOOK LIKE FUN...
EITHER WAY, THEY'RE SERIOUSLY ORGANISED HERE...
THEY ARE, BUT I DON'T THINK THEY'VE BEEN IN THIS TOWN LONG. THEY'RE STILL SETTLING IN.
THIS WAY, NEW PEOPLE! COME IN! COME IN!
COME WITH ME, SAUL... WHAT YOUR FRIENDS ARE ABOUT TO LEARN IS MERELY WHAT I EXPLAINED TO YOU ON THE TRIP HERE...
...AND THE COUNCIL OF SAGES IS EXPECTING YOU IN THE CASTLE.
5

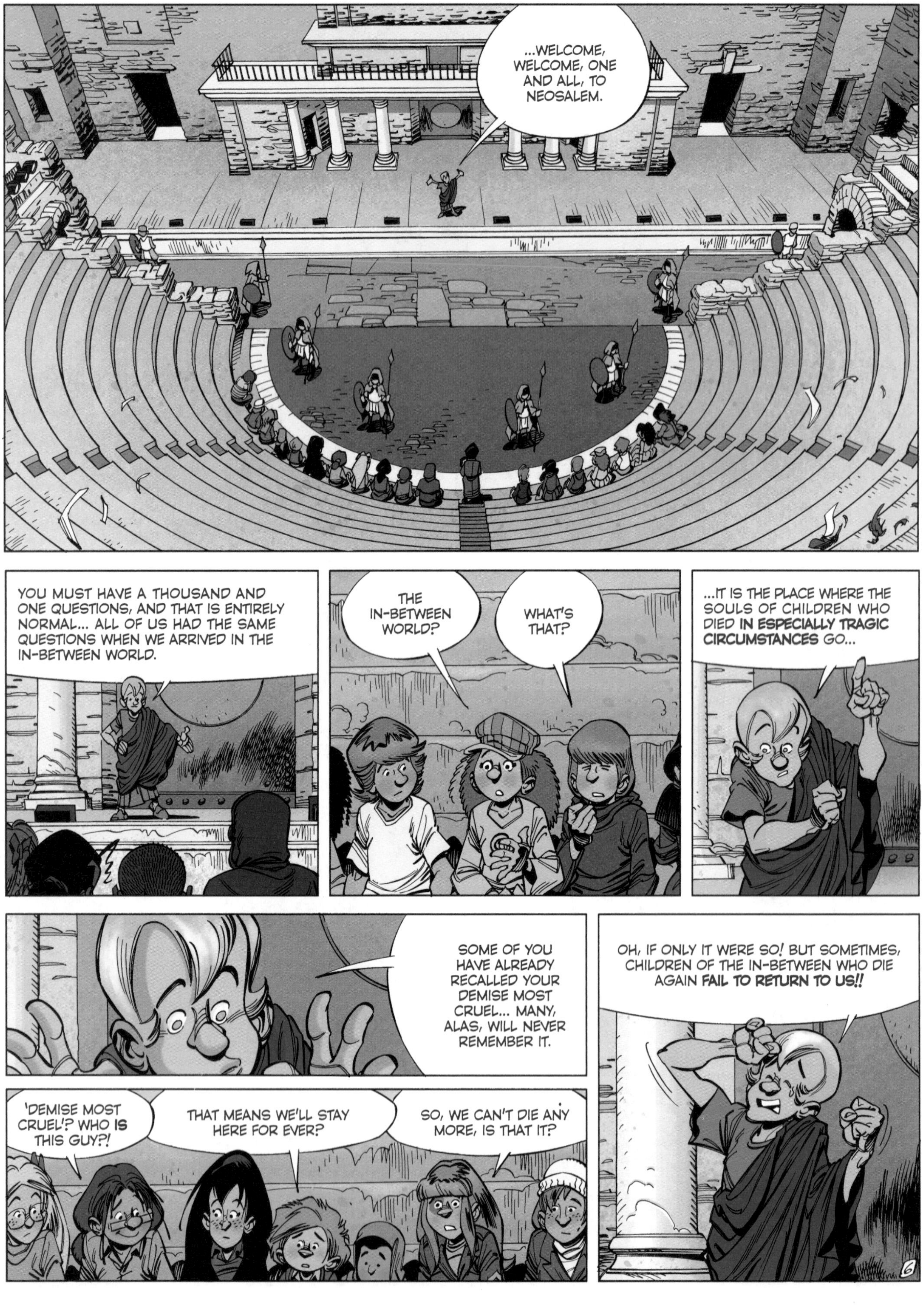
...WELCOME, WELCOME, ONE AND ALL, TO NEOSALEM.
YOU MUST HAVE A THOUSAND AND ONE QUESTIONS, AND THAT IS ENTIRELY NORMAL... ALL OF US HAD THE SAME QUESTIONS WHEN WE ARRIVED IN THE IN-BETWEEN WORLD.
THE IN-BETWEEN WORLD?
WHAT'S THAT?
...IT IS THE PLACE WHERE THE SOULS OF CHILDREN WHO DIED **IN ESPECIALLY TRAGIC CIRCUMSTANCES** GO...
SOME OF YOU HAVE ALREADY RECALLED YOUR DEMISE MOST CRUEL... MANY, ALAS, WILL NEVER REMEMBER IT.
'DEMISE MOST CRUEL'? WHO **IS** THIS GUY?!
THAT MEANS WE'LL STAY HERE FOR EVER?
SO, WE CAN'T DIE ANY MORE, IS THAT IT?
OH, IF ONLY IT WERE SO! BUT SOMETIMES, CHILDREN OF THE IN-BETWEEN WHO DIE AGAIN **FAIL TO RETURN TO US!!**

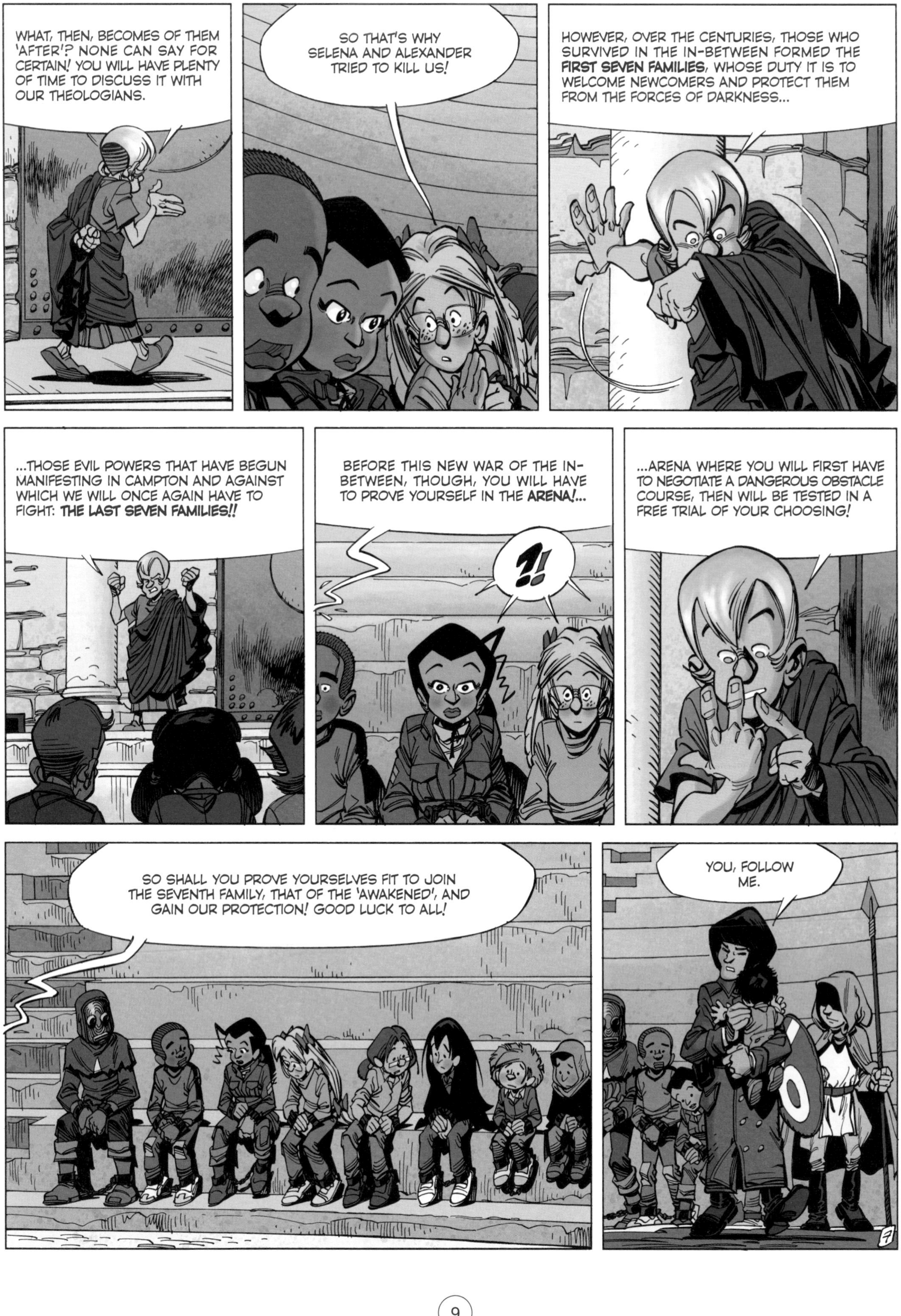
WHAT, THEN, BECOMES OF THEM 'AFTER'? NONE CAN SAY FOR CERTAIN! YOU WILL HAVE PLENTY OF TIME TO DISCUSS IT WITH OUR THEOLOGIANS.
SO THAT'S WHY SELENA AND ALEXANDER TRIED TO KILL US!
HOWEVER, OVER THE CENTURIES, THOSE WHO SURVIVED IN THE IN-BETWEEN FORMED THE **FIRST SEVEN FAMILIES**, WHOSE DUTY IT IS TO WELCOME NEWCOMERS AND PROTECT THEM FROM THE FORCES OF DARKNESS...
...THOSE EVIL POWERS THAT HAVE BEGUN MANIFESTING IN CAMPTON AND AGAINST WHICH WE WILL ONCE AGAIN HAVE TO FIGHT: **THE LAST SEVEN FAMILIES!!**
BEFORE THIS NEW WAR OF THE IN-BETWEEN, THOUGH, YOU WILL HAVE TO PROVE YOURSELF IN THE **ARENA!...**
?!
...ARENA WHERE YOU WILL FIRST HAVE TO NEGOTIATE A DANGEROUS OBSTACLE COURSE, THEN WILL BE TESTED IN A FREE TRIAL OF YOUR CHOOSING!
SO SHALL YOU PROVE YOURSELVES FIT TO JOIN THE SEVENTH FAMILY, THAT OF THE 'AWAKENED', AND GAIN OUR PROTECTION! GOOD LUCK TO ALL!
YOU, FOLLOW ME.

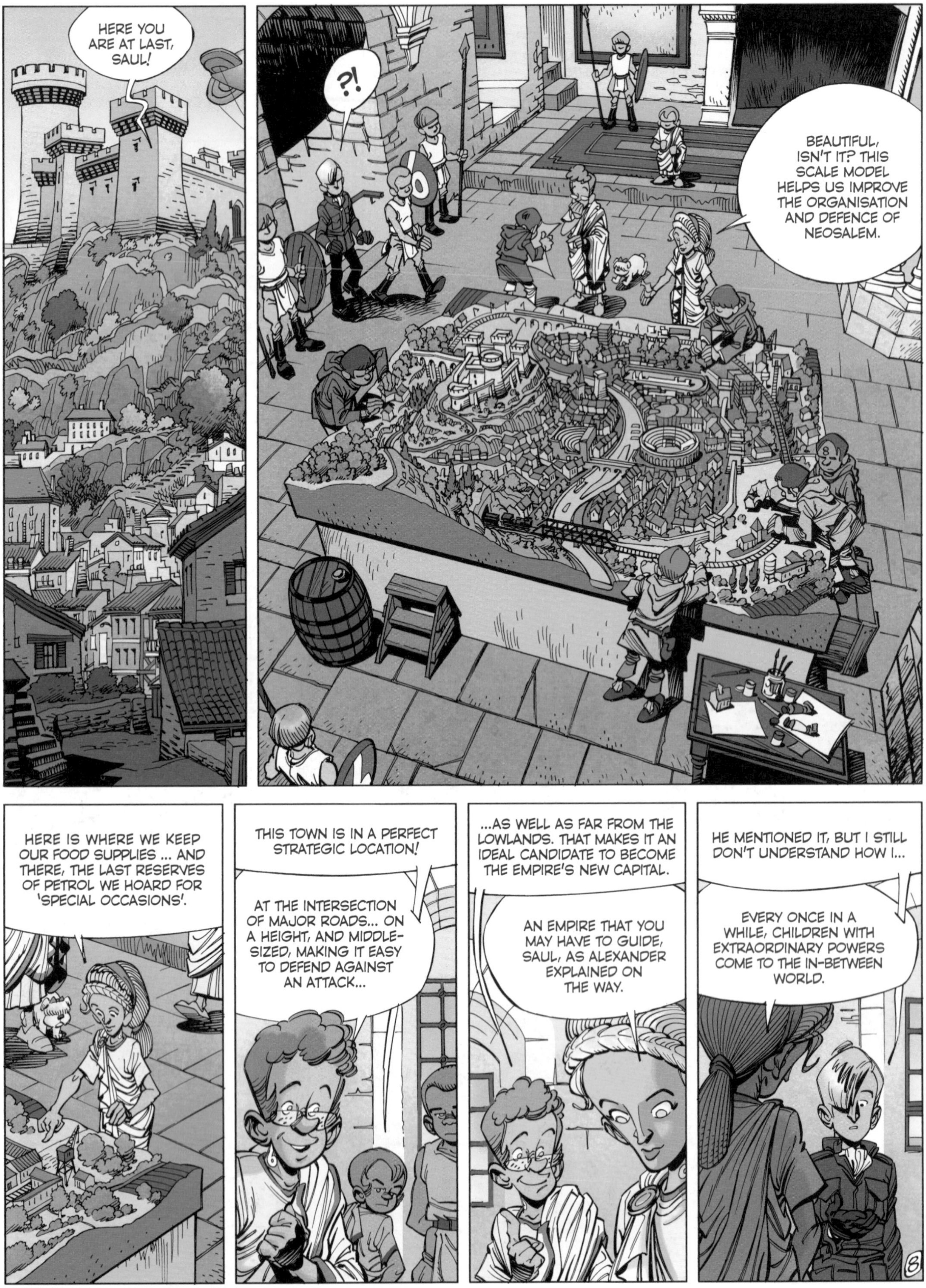
HERE YOU ARE AT LAST, SAUL!
?!
BEAUTIFUL, ISN'T IT? THIS SCALE MODEL HELPS US IMPROVE THE ORGANISATION AND DEFENCE OF NEOSALEM.
HERE IS WHERE WE KEEP OUR FOOD SUPPLIES ... AND THERE, THE LAST RESERVES OF PETROL WE HOARD FOR 'SPECIAL OCCASIONS'.
THIS TOWN IS IN A PERFECT STRATEGIC LOCATION!
AT THE INTERSECTION OF MAJOR ROADS... ON A HEIGHT, AND MIDDLE-SIZED, MAKING IT EASY TO DEFEND AGAINST AN ATTACK...
...AS WELL AS FAR FROM THE LOWLANDS. THAT MAKES IT AN IDEAL CANDIDATE TO BECOME THE EMPIRE'S NEW CAPITAL.
AN EMPIRE THAT YOU MAY HAVE TO GUIDE, SAUL, AS ALEXANDER EXPLAINED ON THE WAY.
HE MENTIONED IT, BUT I STILL DON'T UNDERSTAND HOW I...
EVERY ONCE IN A WHILE, CHILDREN WITH EXTRAORDINARY POWERS COME TO THE IN-BETWEEN WORLD.
8

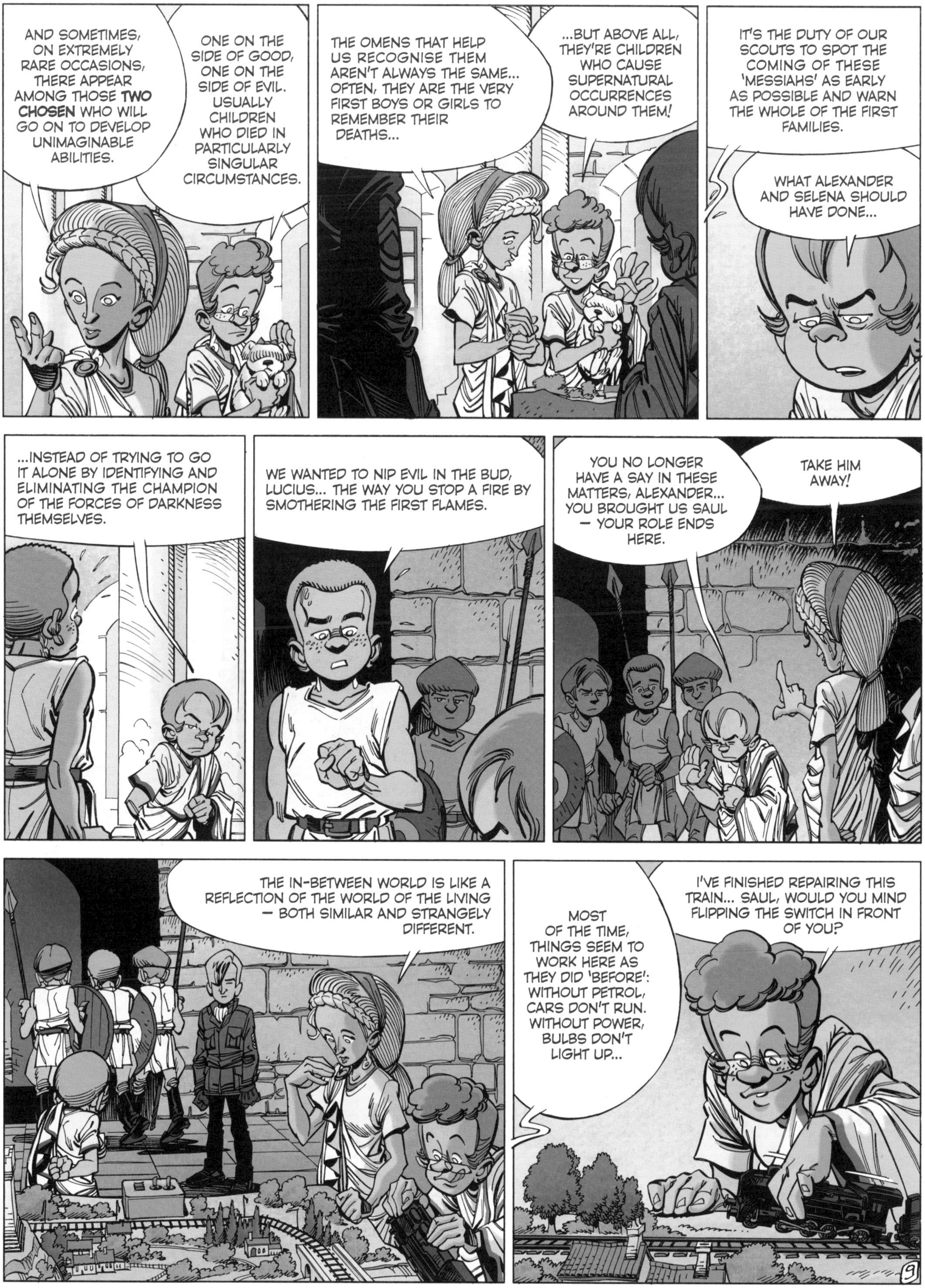
AND SOMETIMES, ON EXTREMELY RARE OCCASIONS, THERE APPEAR AMONG THOSE **TWO CHOSEN** WHO WILL GO ON TO DEVELOP UNIMAGINABLE ABILITIES.
ONE ON THE SIDE OF GOOD, ONE ON THE SIDE OF EVIL. USUALLY CHILDREN WHO DIED IN PARTICULARLY SINGULAR CIRCUMSTANCES.
THE OMENS THAT HELP US RECOGNISE THEM AREN'T ALWAYS THE SAME... OFTEN, THEY ARE THE VERY FIRST BOYS OR GIRLS TO REMEMBER THEIR DEATHS...
...BUT ABOVE ALL, THEY'RE CHILDREN WHO CAUSE SUPERNATURAL OCCURRENCES AROUND THEM!
IT'S THE DUTY OF OUR SCOUTS TO SPOT THE COMING OF THESE 'MESSIAHS' AS EARLY AS POSSIBLE AND WARN THE WHOLE OF THE FIRST FAMILIES.
WHAT ALEXANDER AND SELENA SHOULD HAVE DONE...
...INSTEAD OF TRYING TO GO IT ALONE BY IDENTIFYING AND ELIMINATING THE CHAMPION OF THE FORCES OF DARKNESS THEMSELVES.
WE WANTED TO NIP EVIL IN THE BUD, LUCIUS... THE WAY YOU STOP A FIRE BY SMOTHERING THE FIRST FLAMES.
YOU NO LONGER HAVE A SAY IN THESE MATTERS, ALEXANDER... YOU BROUGHT US SAUL — YOUR ROLE ENDS HERE.
TAKE HIM AWAY!
THE IN-BETWEEN WORLD IS LIKE A REFLECTION OF THE WORLD OF THE LIVING — BOTH SIMILAR AND STRANGELY DIFFERENT.
MOST OF THE TIME, THINGS SEEM TO WORK HERE AS THEY DID 'BEFORE': WITHOUT PETROL, CARS DON'T RUN. WITHOUT POWER, BULBS DON'T LIGHT UP...
I'VE FINISHED REPAIRING THIS TRAIN... SAUL, WOULD YOU MIND FLIPPING THE SWITCH IN FRONT OF YOU?
9

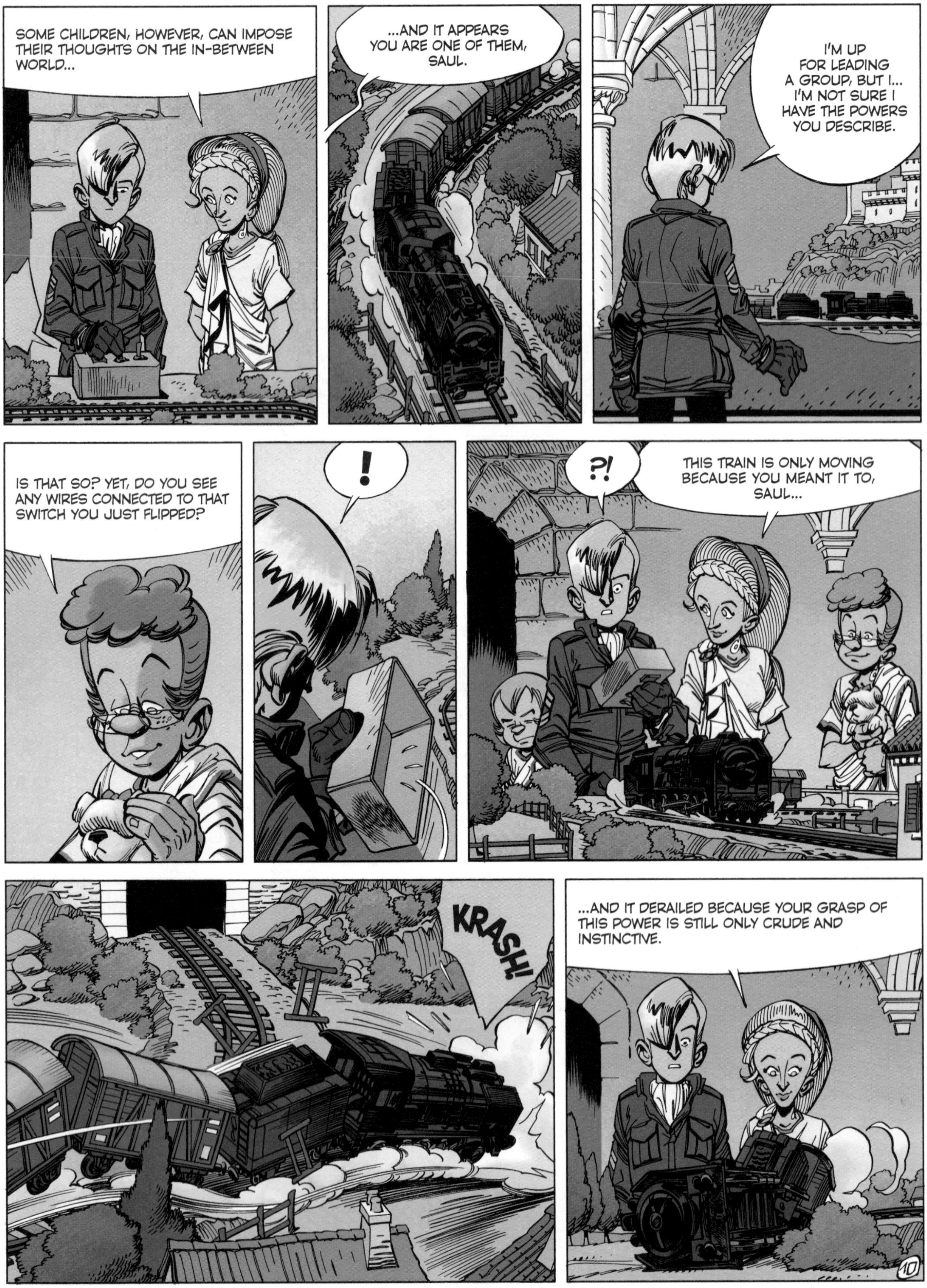
SOME CHILDREN, HOWEVER, CAN IMPOSE THEIR THOUGHTS ON THE IN-BETWEEN WORLD...
...AND IT APPEARS YOU ARE ONE OF THEM, SAUL.
I'M UP FOR LEADING A GROUP, BUT I... I'M NOT SURE I HAVE THE POWERS YOU DESCRIBE.
IS THAT SO? YET, DO YOU SEE ANY WIRES CONNECTED TO THAT SWITCH YOU JUST FLIPPED?
!
?!
THIS TRAIN IS ONLY MOVING BECAUSE YOU MEANT IT TO, SAUL...
KRASH!
...AND IT DERAILED BECAUSE YOUR GRASP OF THIS POWER IS STILL ONLY CRUDE AND INSTINCTIVE.
10

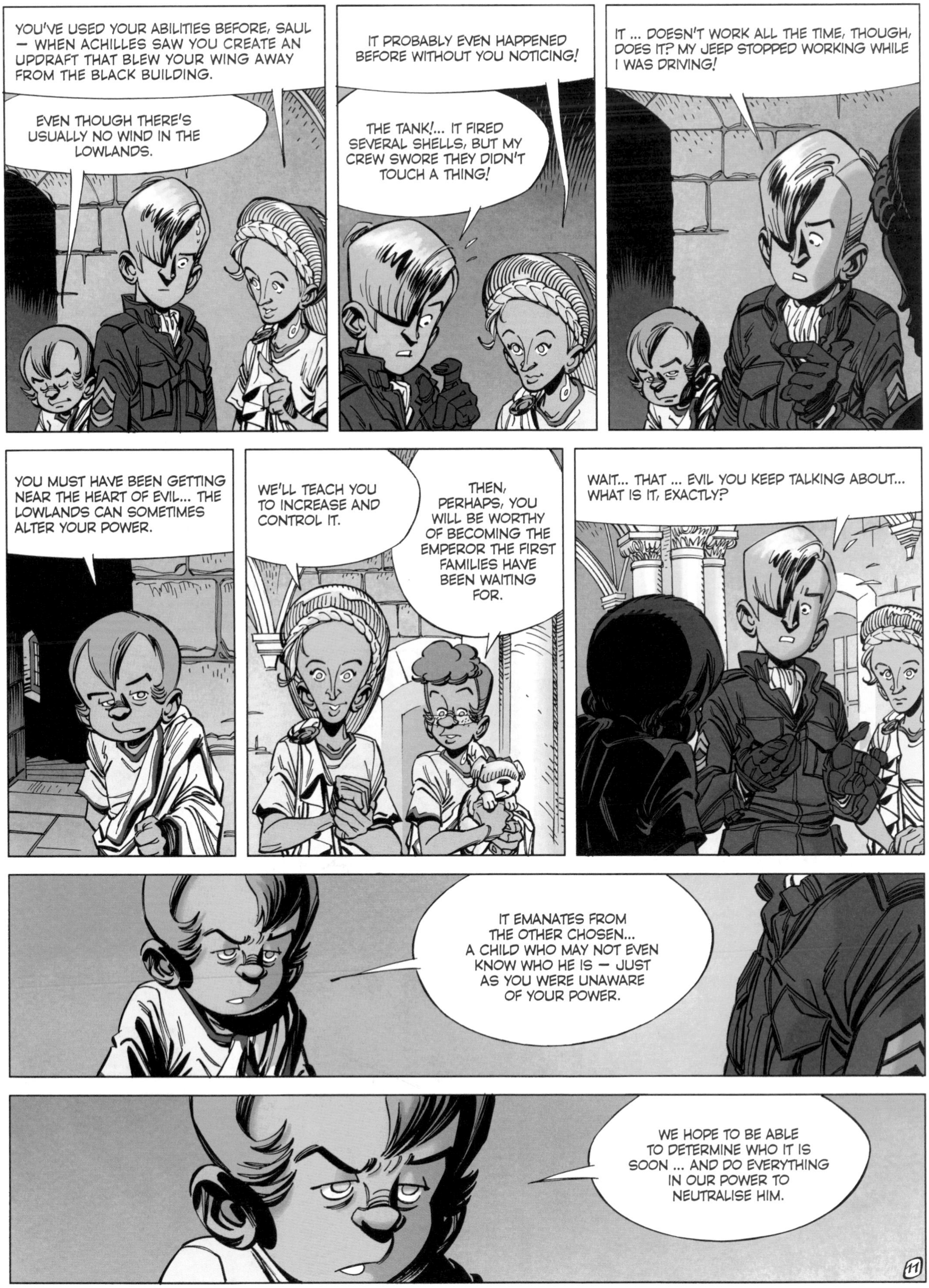
YOU'VE USED YOUR ABILITIES BEFORE, SAUL — WHEN ACHILLES SAW YOU CREATE AN UPDRAFT THAT BLEW YOUR WING AWAY FROM THE BLACK BUILDING.
EVEN THOUGH THERE'S USUALLY NO WIND IN THE LOWLANDS.
IT PROBABLY EVEN HAPPENED BEFORE WITHOUT YOU NOTICING!
THE TANK!... IT FIRED SEVERAL SHELLS, BUT MY CREW SWORE THEY DIDN'T TOUCH A THING!
IT ... DOESN'T WORK ALL THE TIME, THOUGH, DOES IT? MY JEEP STOPPED WORKING WHILE I WAS DRIVING!
YOU MUST HAVE BEEN GETTING NEAR THE HEART OF EVIL... THE LOWLANDS CAN SOMETIMES ALTER YOUR POWER.
WE'LL TEACH YOU TO INCREASE AND CONTROL IT.
THEN, PERHAPS, YOU WILL BE WORTHY OF BECOMING THE EMPEROR THE FIRST FAMILIES HAVE BEEN WAITING FOR.
WAIT... THAT ... EVIL YOU KEEP TALKING ABOUT... WHAT IS IT, EXACTLY?
IT EMANATES FROM THE OTHER CHOSEN... A CHILD WHO MAY NOT EVEN KNOW WHO HE IS — JUST AS YOU WERE UNAWARE OF YOUR POWER.
WE HOPE TO BE ABLE TO DETERMINE WHO IT IS SOON ... AND DO EVERYTHING IN OUR POWER TO NEUTRALISE HIM.
11

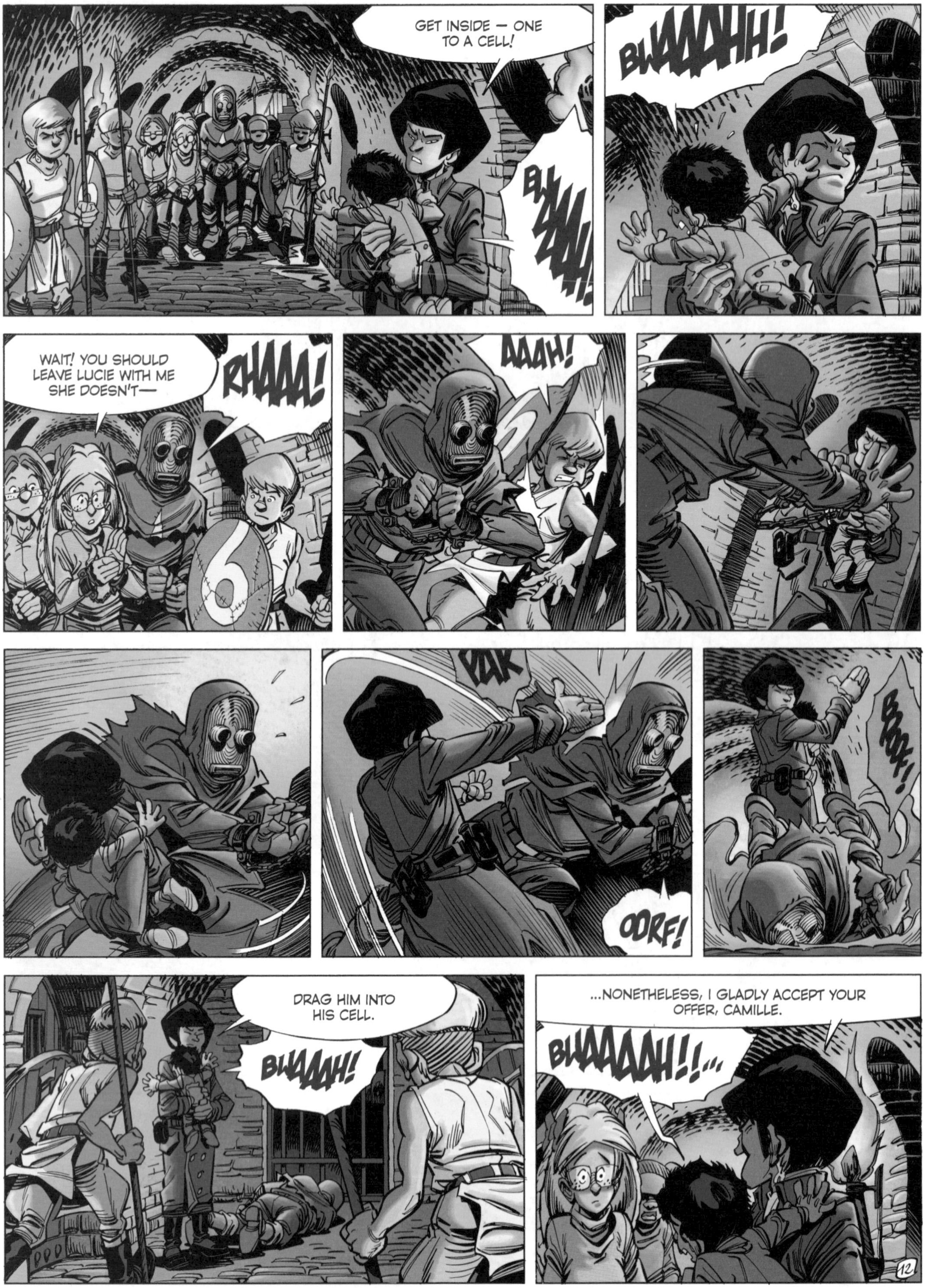
GET INSIDE — ONE TO A CELL!
BWAAAHH!
BWAAAH!
WAIT! YOU SHOULD LEAVE LUCIE WITH ME SHE DOESN'T—
RHAAA!
AAAH!
DAK
BOOOK!
OORF!
DRAG HIM INTO HIS CELL.
BWAAAH!
...NONETHELESS, I GLADLY ACCEPT YOUR OFFER, CAMILLE.
BWAAAAH!!...
12

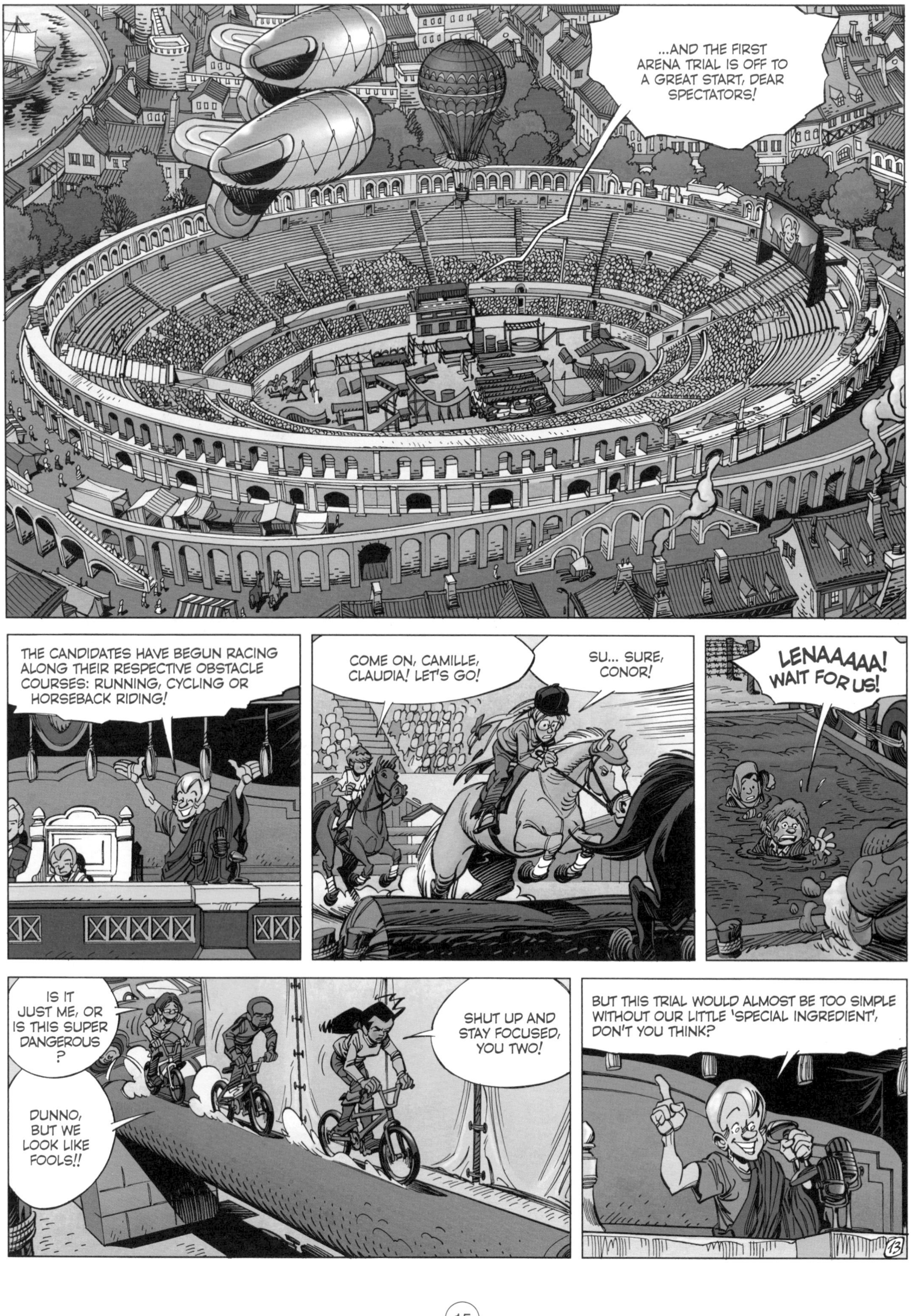
...AND THE FIRST ARENA TRIAL IS OFF TO A GREAT START, DEAR SPECTATORS!
THE CANDIDATES HAVE BEGUN RACING ALONG THEIR RESPECTIVE OBSTACLE COURSES: RUNNING, CYCLING OR HORSEBACK RIDING!
COME ON, CAMILLE, CLAUDIA! LET'S GO!
SU... SURE, CONOR!
LENAAAAA! WAIT FOR US!
IS IT JUST ME, OR IS THIS SUPER DANGEROUS ?
DUNNO, BUT WE LOOK LIKE FOOLS!!
SHUT UP AND STAY FOCUSED, YOU TWO!
BUT THIS TRIAL WOULD ALMOST BE TOO SIMPLE WITHOUT OUR LITTLE 'SPECIAL INGREDIENT', DON'T YOU THINK?
13

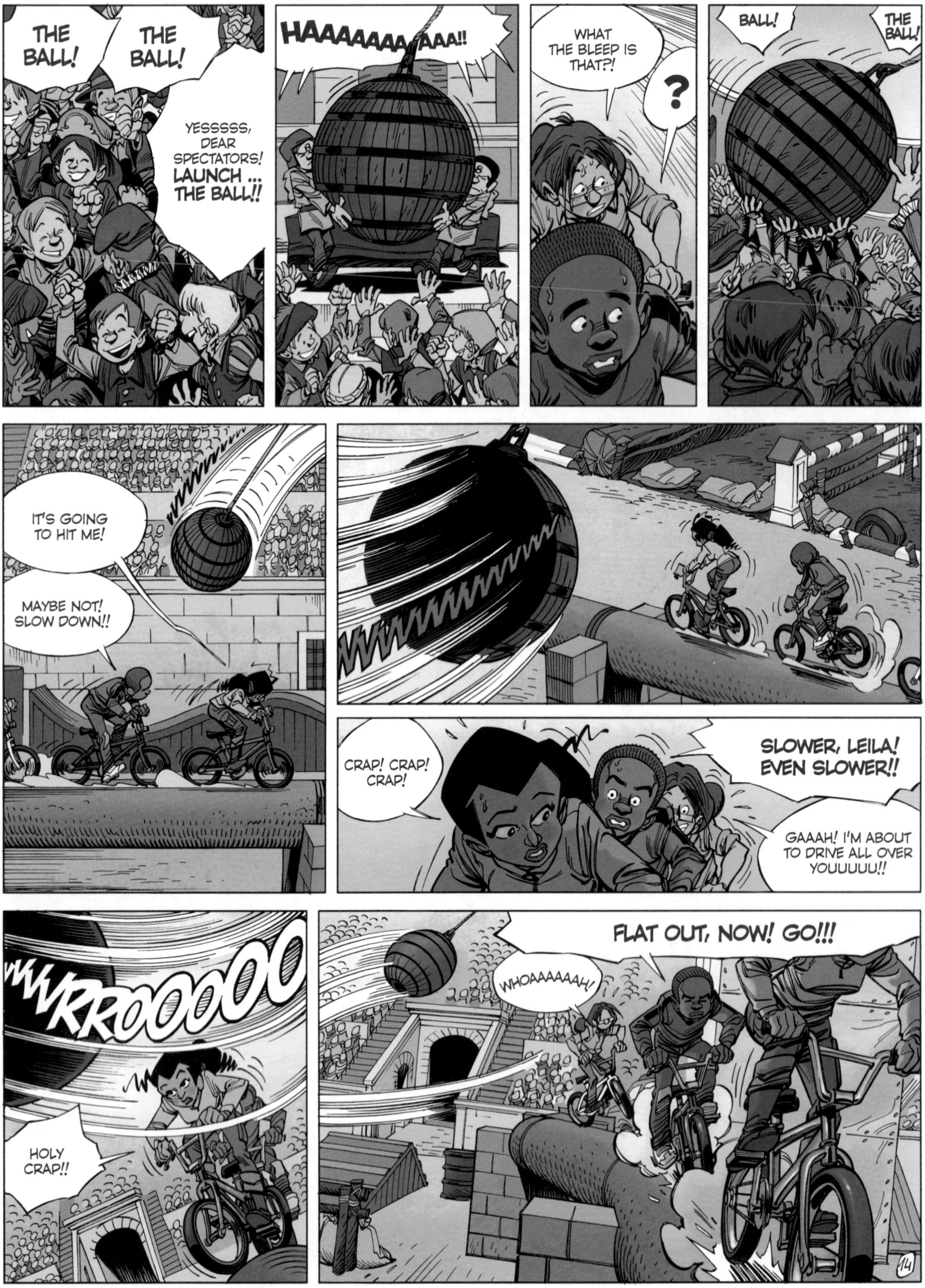
THE BALL!
THE BALL!
YESSSSS, DEAR SPECTATORS! LAUNCH ... THE BALL!!
HAAAAAAAAAAA!!
WHAT THE BLEEP IS THAT?!
?
BALL!
THE BALL!
IT'S GOING TO HIT ME!
MAYBE NOT! SLOW DOWN!!
CRAP! CRAP! CRAP!
SLOWER, LEILA! EVEN SLOWER!!
GAAAH! I'M ABOUT TO DRIVE ALL OVER YOUUUUU!!
WWRROOOOOO
HOLY CRAP!!
FLAT OUT, NOW! GO!!!
WHOAAAAAAH!

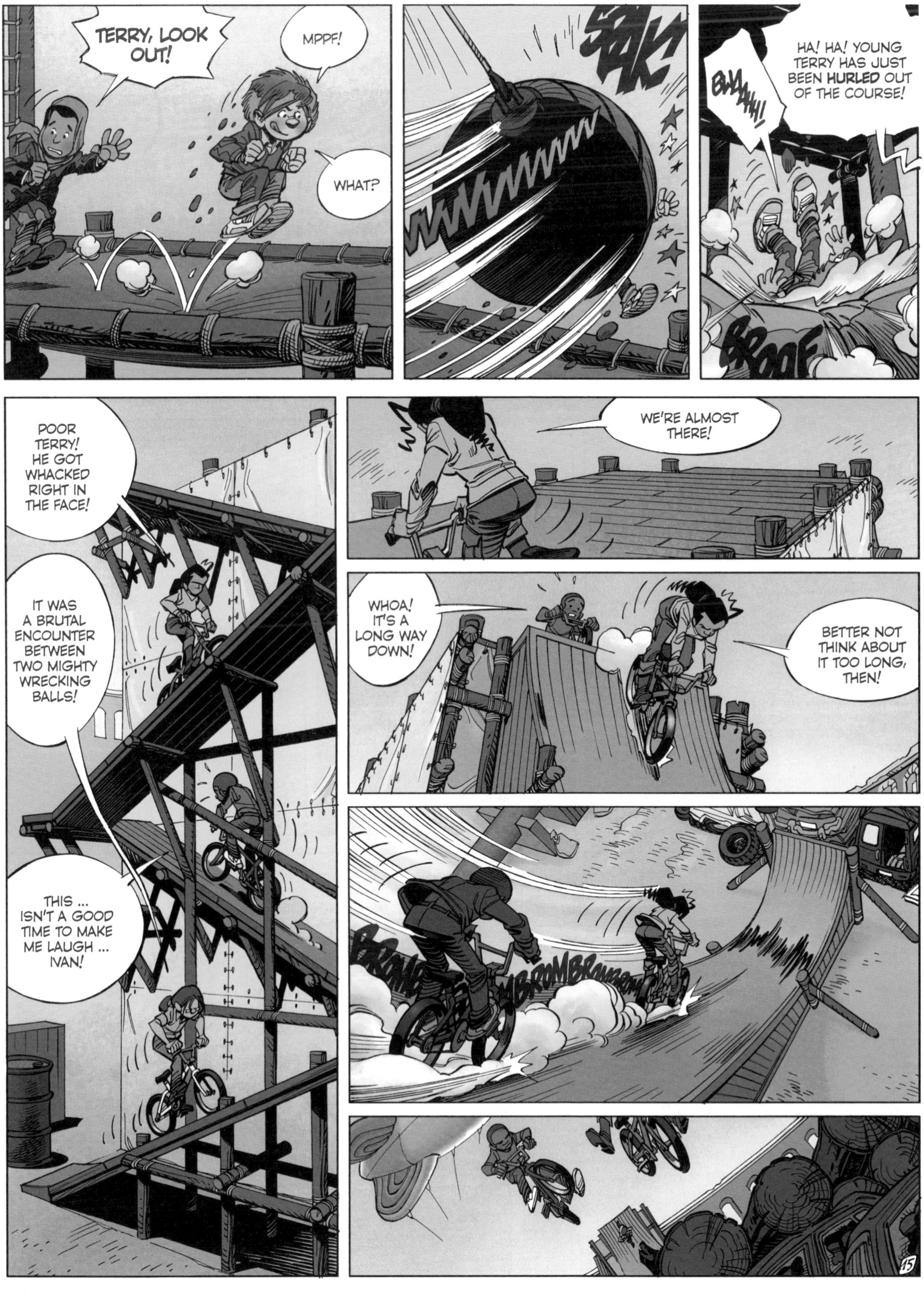
TERRY, LOOK OUT!
MPPF!
WHAT?
HA! HA! YOUNG TERRY HAS JUST BEEN HURLED OUT OF THE COURSE!
BROOF
POOR TERRY! HE GOT WHACKED RIGHT IN THE FACE!
IT WAS A BRUTAL ENCOUNTER BETWEEN TWO MIGHTY WRECKING BALLS!
THIS ... ISN'T A GOOD TIME TO MAKE ME LAUGH ... IVAN!
WE'RE ALMOST THERE!
WHOA! IT'S A LONG WAY DOWN!
BETTER NOT THINK ABOUT IT TOO LONG, THEN!

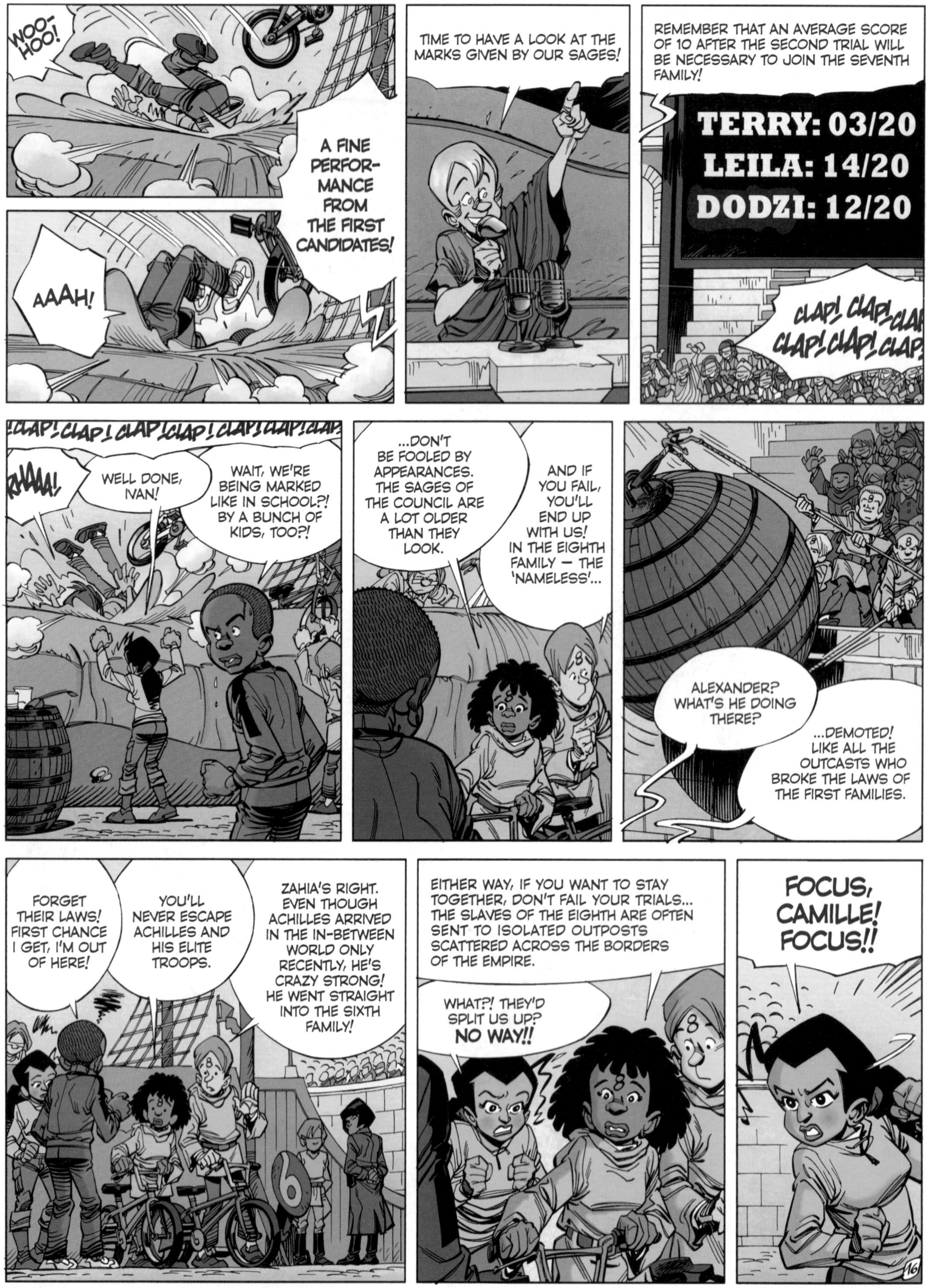
WOO-HOO!
A FINE PERFORMANCE FROM THE FIRST CANDIDATES!
AAAH!
TIME TO HAVE A LOOK AT THE MARKS GIVEN BY OUR SAGES!
REMEMBER THAT AN AVERAGE SCORE OF 10 AFTER THE SECOND TRIAL WILL BE NECESSARY TO JOIN THE SEVENTH FAMILY!
TERRY: 03/20
LEILA: 14/20
DODZI: 12/20
CLAP! CLAP! CLAP! CLAP! CLAP! CLAP!
CLAP! CLAP! CLAP! CLAP! CLAP! CLAP! CLAP!
WELL DONE, IVAN!
WAIT, WE'RE BEING MARKED LIKE IN SCHOOL?! BY A BUNCH OF KIDS, TOO?!
...DON'T BE FOOLED BY APPEARANCES. THE SAGES OF THE COUNCIL ARE A LOT OLDER THAN THEY LOOK.
AND IF YOU FAIL, YOU'LL END UP WITH US! IN THE EIGHTH FAMILY — THE 'NAMELESS'...
ALEXANDER? WHAT'S HE DOING THERE?
...DEMOTED! LIKE ALL THE OUTCASTS WHO BROKE THE LAWS OF THE FIRST FAMILIES.
FORGET THEIR LAWS! FIRST CHANCE I GET, I'M OUT OF HERE!
YOU'LL NEVER ESCAPE ACHILLES AND HIS ELITE TROOPS.
ZAHIA'S RIGHT. EVEN THOUGH ACHILLES ARRIVED IN THE IN-BETWEEN WORLD ONLY RECENTLY, HE'S CRAZY STRONG! HE WENT STRAIGHT INTO THE SIXTH FAMILY!
EITHER WAY, IF YOU WANT TO STAY TOGETHER, DON'T FAIL YOUR TRIALS... THE SLAVES OF THE EIGHTH ARE OFTEN SENT TO ISOLATED OUTPOSTS SCATTERED ACROSS THE BORDERS OF THE EMPIRE.
WHAT?! THEY'D SPLIT US UP? NO WAY!!
FOCUS, CAMILLE! FOCUS!!
16

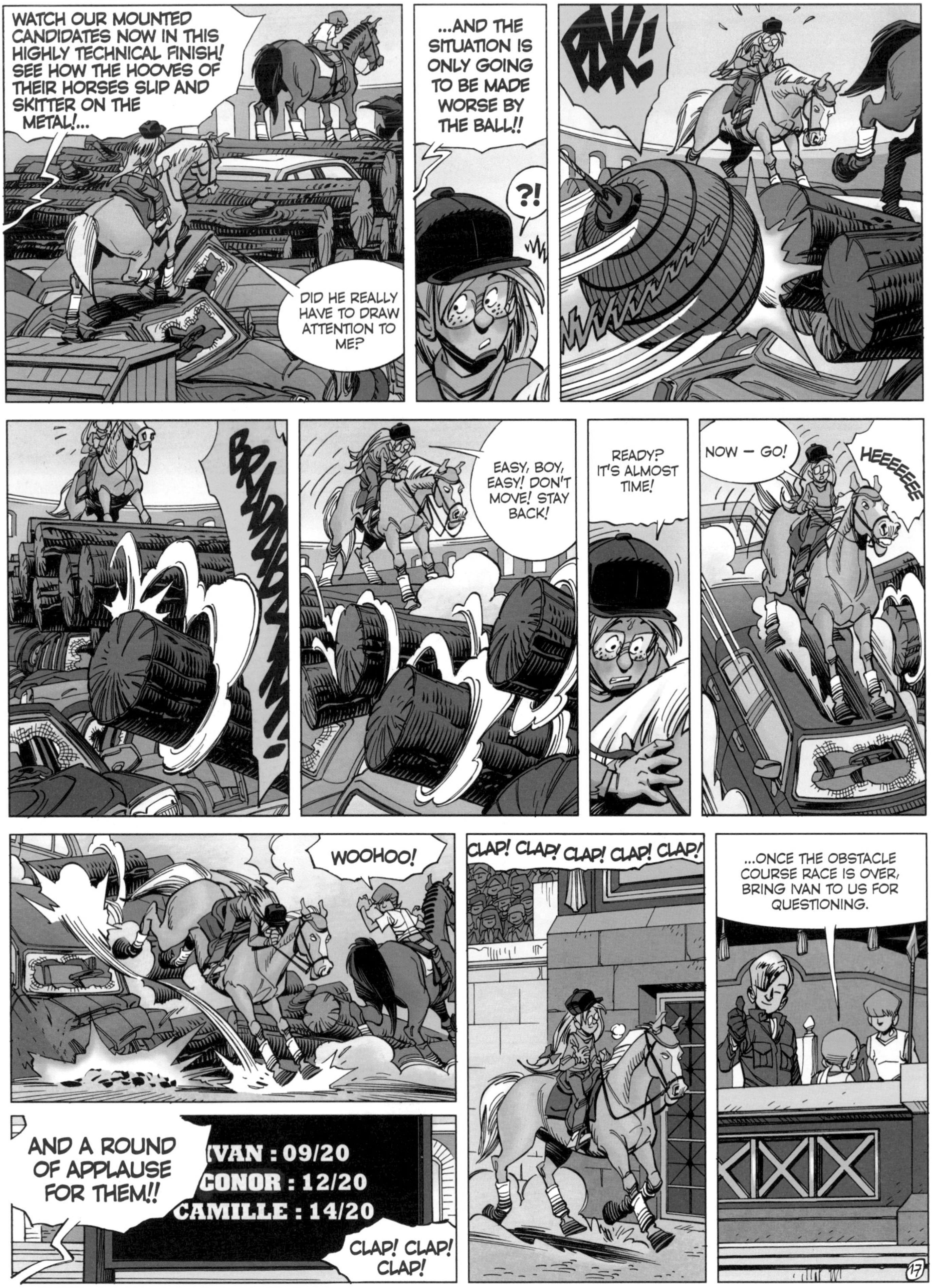
WATCH OUR MOUNTED CANDIDATES NOW IN THIS HIGHLY TECHNICAL FINISH! SEE HOW THE HOOVES OF THEIR HORSES SLIP AND SKITTER ON THE METAL!...
DID HE REALLY HAVE TO DRAW ATTENTION TO ME?
...AND THE SITUATION IS ONLY GOING TO BE MADE WORSE BY THE BALL!!
?!
PZK!
EASY, BOY, EASY! DON'T MOVE! STAY BACK!
READY? IT'S ALMOST TIME!
NOW – GO!
HEEEEEEE
WOOHOO!
AND A ROUND OF APPLAUSE FOR THEM!!
IVAN : 09/20
CONOR : 12/20
CAMILLE : 14/20
CLAP! CLAP! CLAP!
CLAP! CLAP! CLAP! CLAP! CLAP!
...ONCE THE OBSTACLE COURSE RACE IS OVER, BRING IVAN TO US FOR QUESTIONING.
17

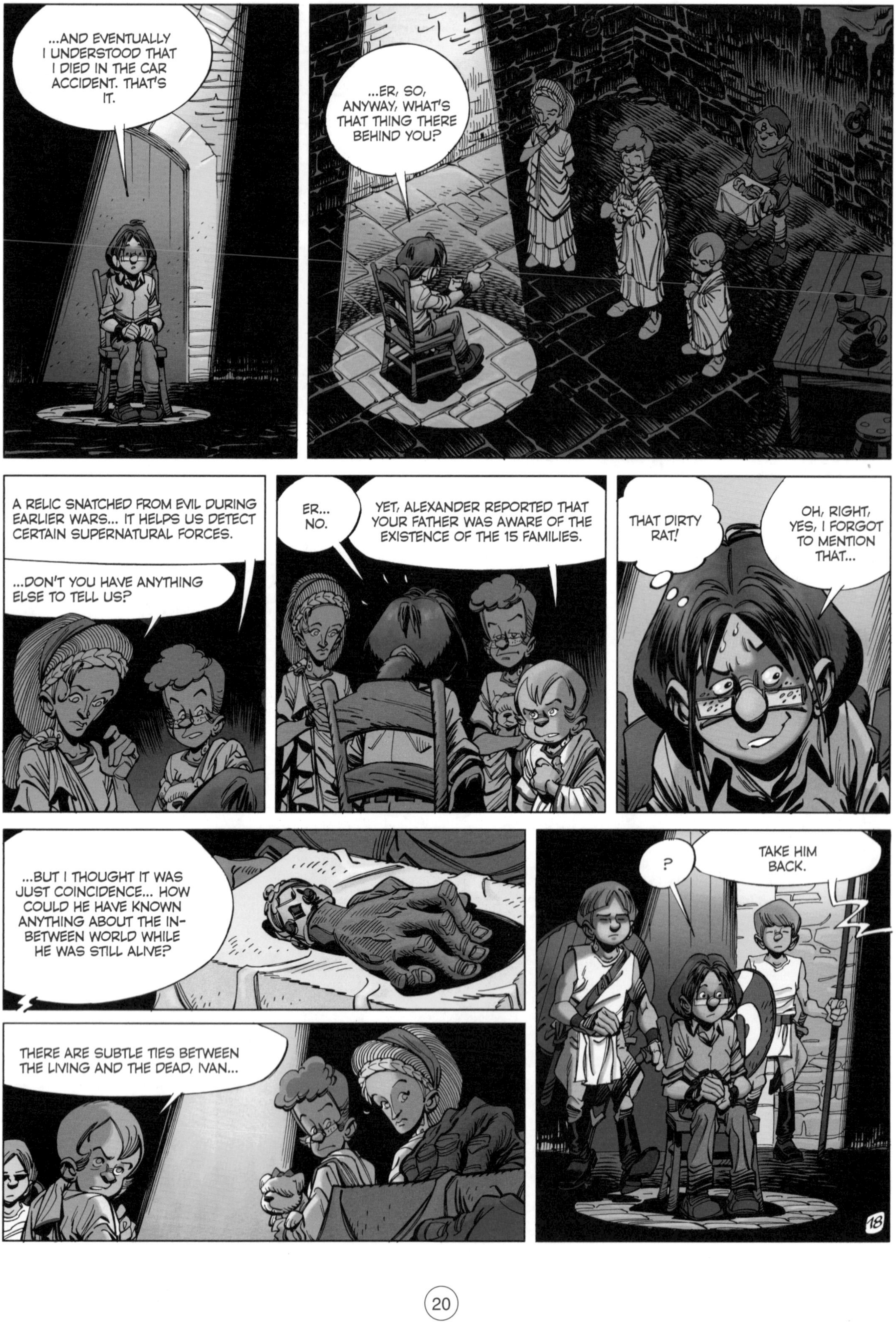
...AND EVENTUALLY I UNDERSTOOD THAT I DIED IN THE CAR ACCIDENT. THAT'S IT.
...ER, SO, ANYWAY, WHAT'S THAT THING THERE BEHIND YOU?
A RELIC SNATCHED FROM EVIL DURING EARLIER WARS... IT HELPS US DETECT CERTAIN SUPERNATURAL FORCES.
...DON'T YOU HAVE ANYTHING ELSE TO TELL US?
ER... NO.
YET, ALEXANDER REPORTED THAT YOUR FATHER WAS AWARE OF THE EXISTENCE OF THE 15 FAMILIES.
THAT DIRTY RAT!
OH, RIGHT, YES, I FORGOT TO MENTION THAT...
...BUT I THOUGHT IT WAS JUST COINCIDENCE... HOW COULD HE HAVE KNOWN ANYTHING ABOUT THE IN-BETWEEN WORLD WHILE HE WAS STILL ALIVE?
THERE ARE SUBTLE TIES BETWEEN THE LIVING AND THE DEAD, IVAN...
?
TAKE HIM BACK.
18

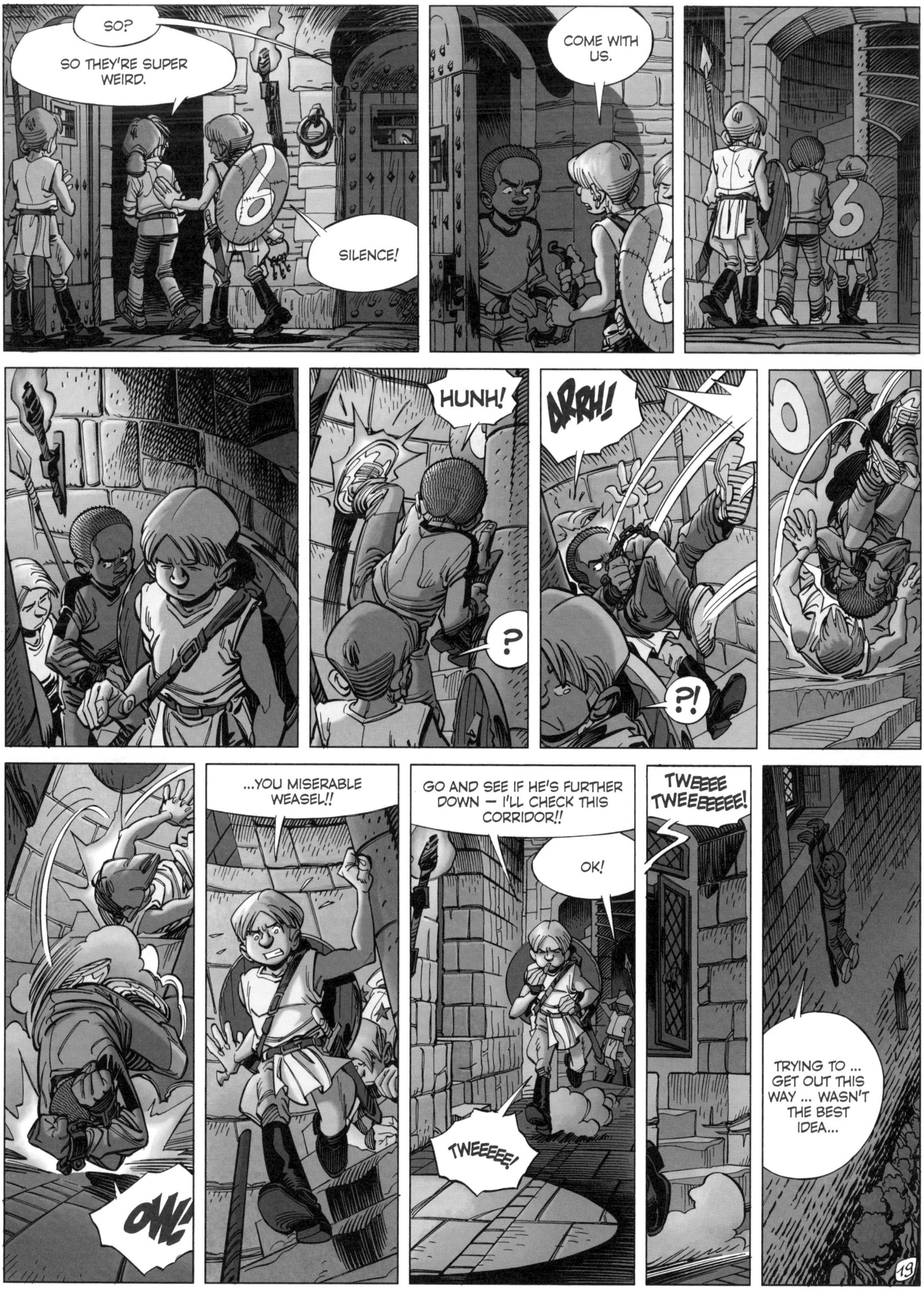
SO?
SO THEY'RE SUPER WEIRD.
SILENCE!
COME WITH US.
HUNH!
?
ARRH!
?!
OW!
...YOU MISERABLE WEASEL!!
GO AND SEE IF HE'S FURTHER DOWN — I'LL CHECK THIS CORRIDOR!!
OK!
TWEEEEE!
TWEEEE TWEEEEEEE!
TRYING TO ... GET OUT THIS WAY ... WASN'T THE BEST IDEA...
19

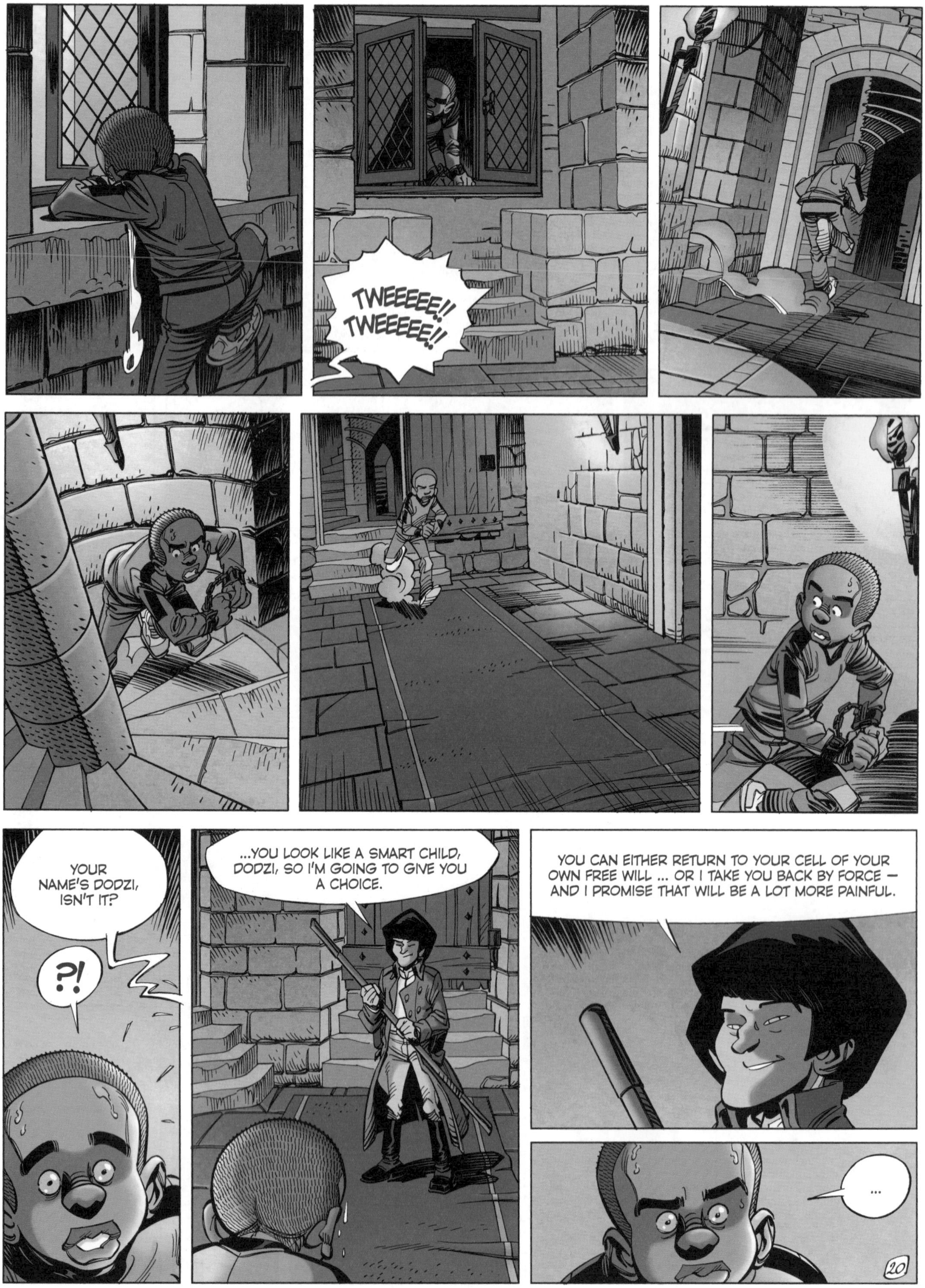
TWEEEEE!! TWEEEEE!!
YOUR NAME'S DODZI, ISN'T IT?
?!
...YOU LOOK LIKE A SMART CHILD, DODZI, SO I'M GOING TO GIVE YOU A CHOICE.
YOU CAN EITHER RETURN TO YOUR CELL OF YOUR OWN FREE WILL ... OR I TAKE YOU BACK BY FORCE — AND I PROMISE THAT WILL BE A LOT MORE PAINFUL.
...
20

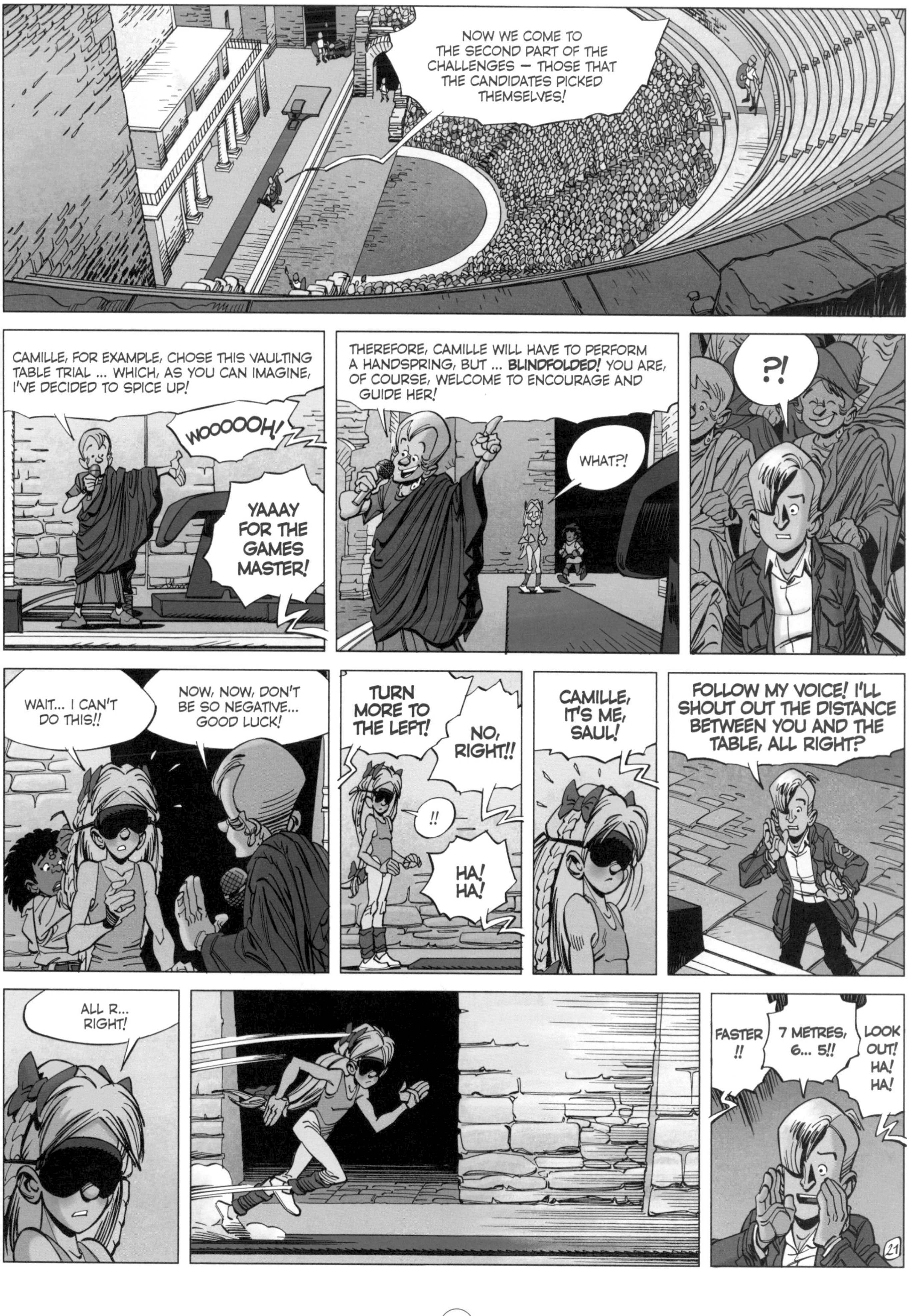
NOW WE COME TO THE SECOND PART OF THE CHALLENGES — THOSE THAT THE CANDIDATES PICKED THEMSELVES!
CAMILLE, FOR EXAMPLE, CHOSE THIS VAULTING TABLE TRIAL ... WHICH, AS YOU CAN IMAGINE, I'VE DECIDED TO SPICE UP!
WOOOOOH!
YAAAY FOR THE GAMES MASTER!
THEREFORE, CAMILLE WILL HAVE TO PERFORM A HANDSPRING, BUT ... BLINDFOLDED! YOU ARE, OF COURSE, WELCOME TO ENCOURAGE AND GUIDE HER!
WHAT?!
?!
WAIT... I CAN'T DO THIS!!
NOW, NOW, DON'T BE SO NEGATIVE... GOOD LUCK!
TURN MORE TO THE LEFT!
NO, RIGHT!!
!!
HA! HA!
CAMILLE, IT'S ME, SAUL!
FOLLOW MY VOICE! I'LL SHOUT OUT THE DISTANCE BETWEEN YOU AND THE TABLE, ALL RIGHT?
ALL R... RIGHT!
FASTER !!
7 METRES, 6... 5!!
LOOK OUT! HA! HA!
21

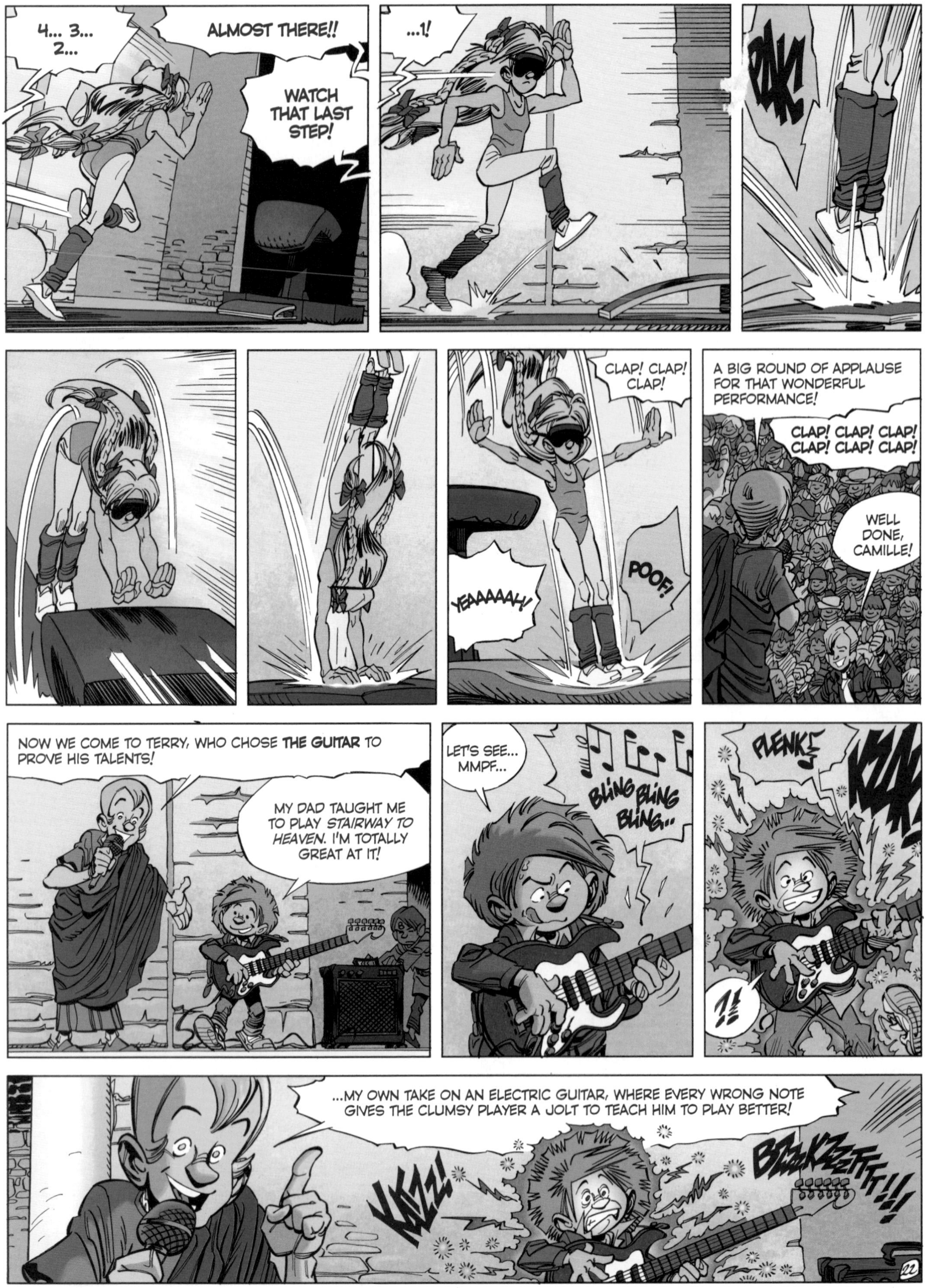

4... 3... 2...
ALMOST THERE!!
WATCH THAT LAST STEP!
...1!
CLAP! CLAP! CLAP!
YEAAAAAH!
POOF!
A BIG ROUND OF APPLAUSE FOR THAT WONDERFUL PERFORMANCE!
CLAP! CLAP! CLAP! CLAP! CLAP! CLAP!
WELL DONE, CAMILLE!
NOW WE COME TO TERRY, WHO CHOSE THE GUITAR TO PROVE HIS TALENTS!
MY DAD TAUGHT ME TO PLAY STAIRWAY TO HEAVEN. I'M TOTALLY GREAT AT IT!
LET'S SEE... MMPF...
BLING BLING BLING...
PLENK!
...MY OWN TAKE ON AN ELECTRIC GUITAR, WHERE EVERY WRONG NOTE GIVES THE CLUMSY PLAYER A JOLT TO TEACH HIM TO PLAY BETTER!

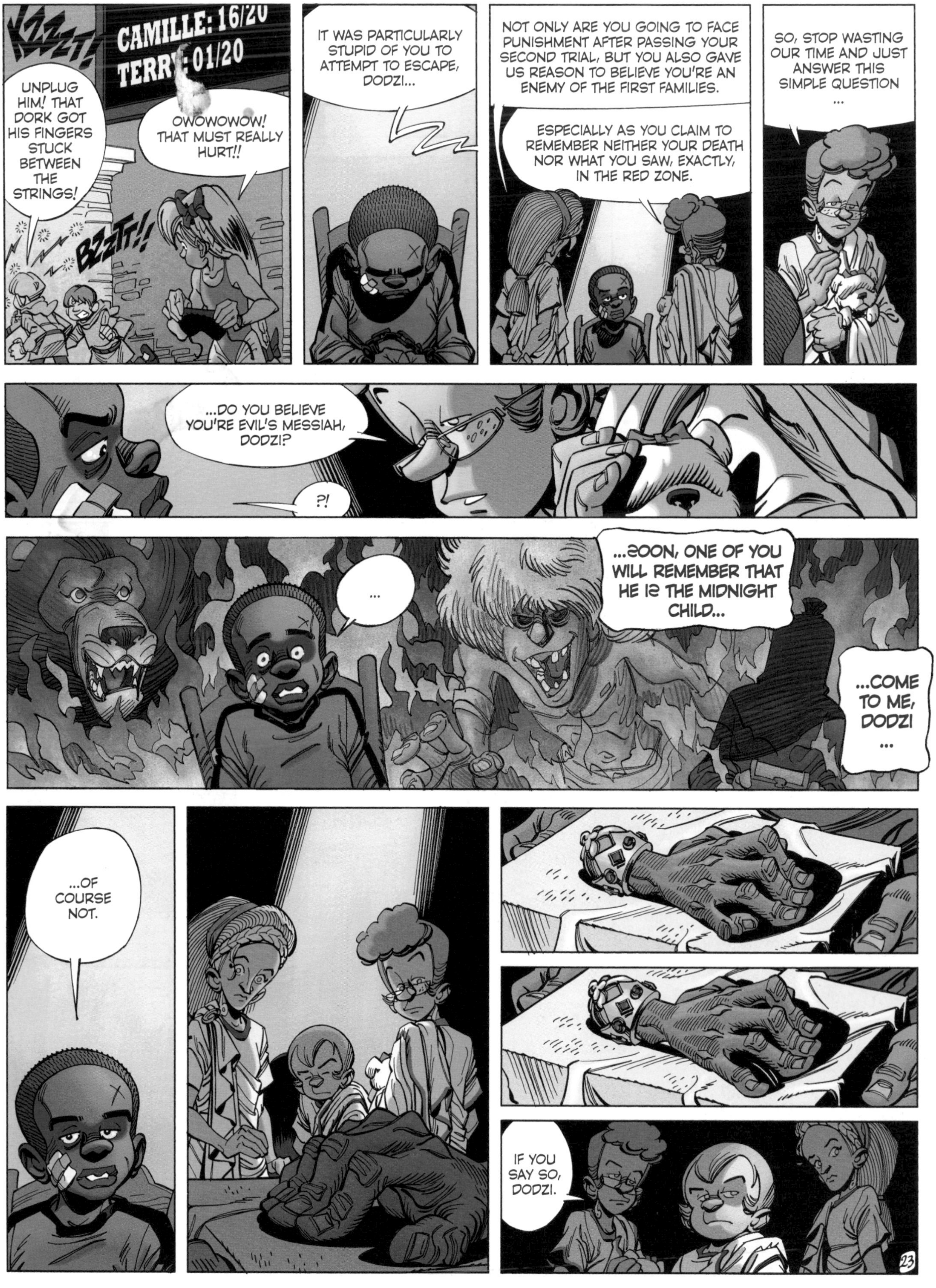
KZZZT!
CAMILLE: 16/20
TERRY: 01/20
UNPLUG HIM! THAT DORK GOT HIS FINGERS STUCK BETWEEN THE STRINGS!
OWOWOWOW! THAT MUST REALLY HURT!!
BZZTT!!
IT WAS PARTICULARLY STUPID OF YOU TO ATTEMPT TO ESCAPE, DODZI...
NOT ONLY ARE YOU GOING TO FACE PUNISHMENT AFTER PASSING YOUR SECOND TRIAL, BUT YOU ALSO GAVE US REASON TO BELIEVE YOU'RE AN ENEMY OF THE FIRST FAMILIES.
ESPECIALLY AS YOU CLAIM TO REMEMBER NEITHER YOUR DEATH NOR WHAT YOU SAW, EXACTLY, IN THE RED ZONE.
SO, STOP WASTING OUR TIME AND JUST ANSWER THIS SIMPLE QUESTION ...
...DO YOU BELIEVE YOU'RE EVIL'S MESSIAH, DODZI?
?!
...
...SOON, ONE OF YOU WILL REMEMBER THAT HE IS THE MIDNIGHT CHILD...
...COME TO ME, DODZI ...
...OF COURSE NOT.
IF YOU SAY SO, DODZI.
23

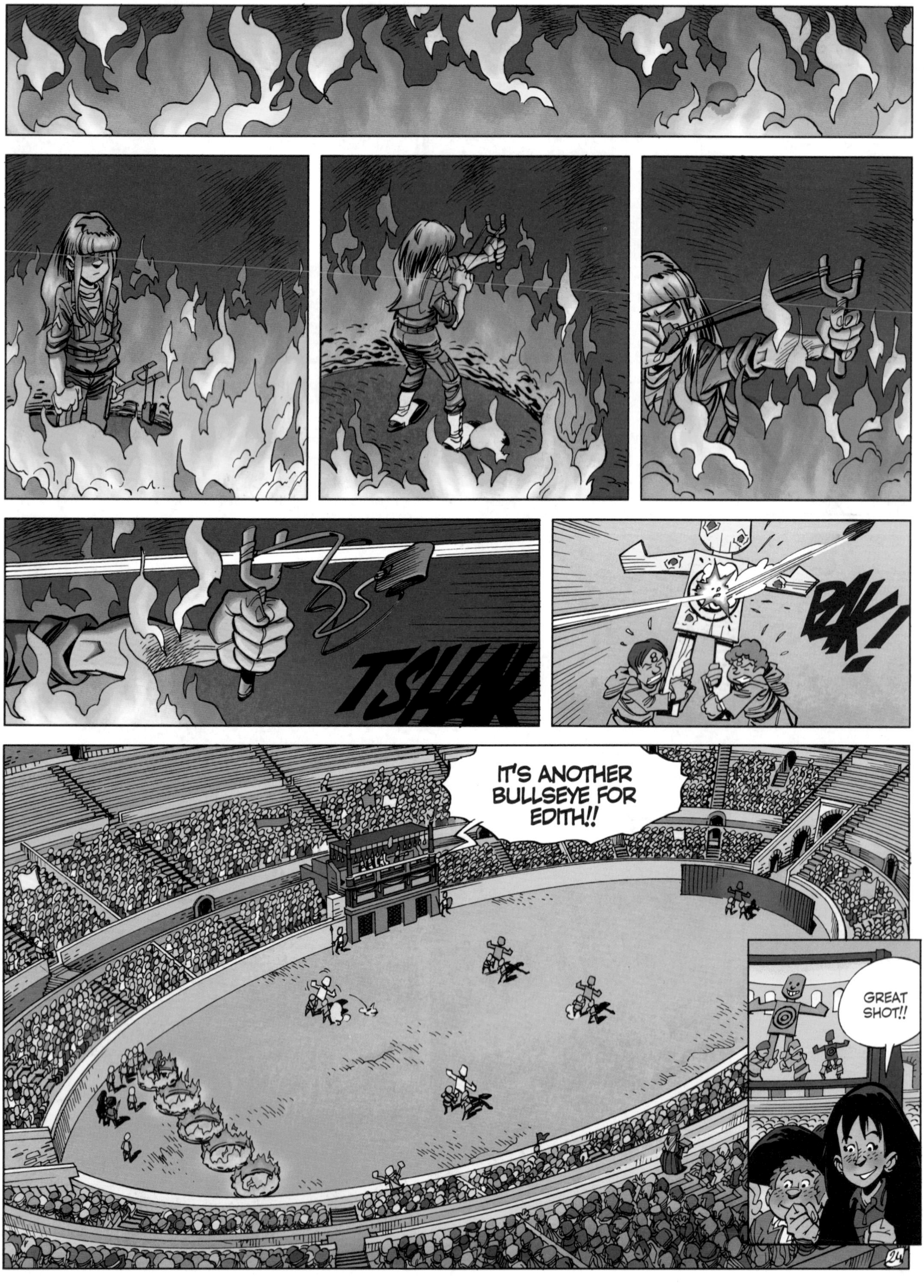
TSHAK
BAK!
IT'S ANOTHER BULLSEYE FOR EDITH!!
GREAT SHOT!!
24

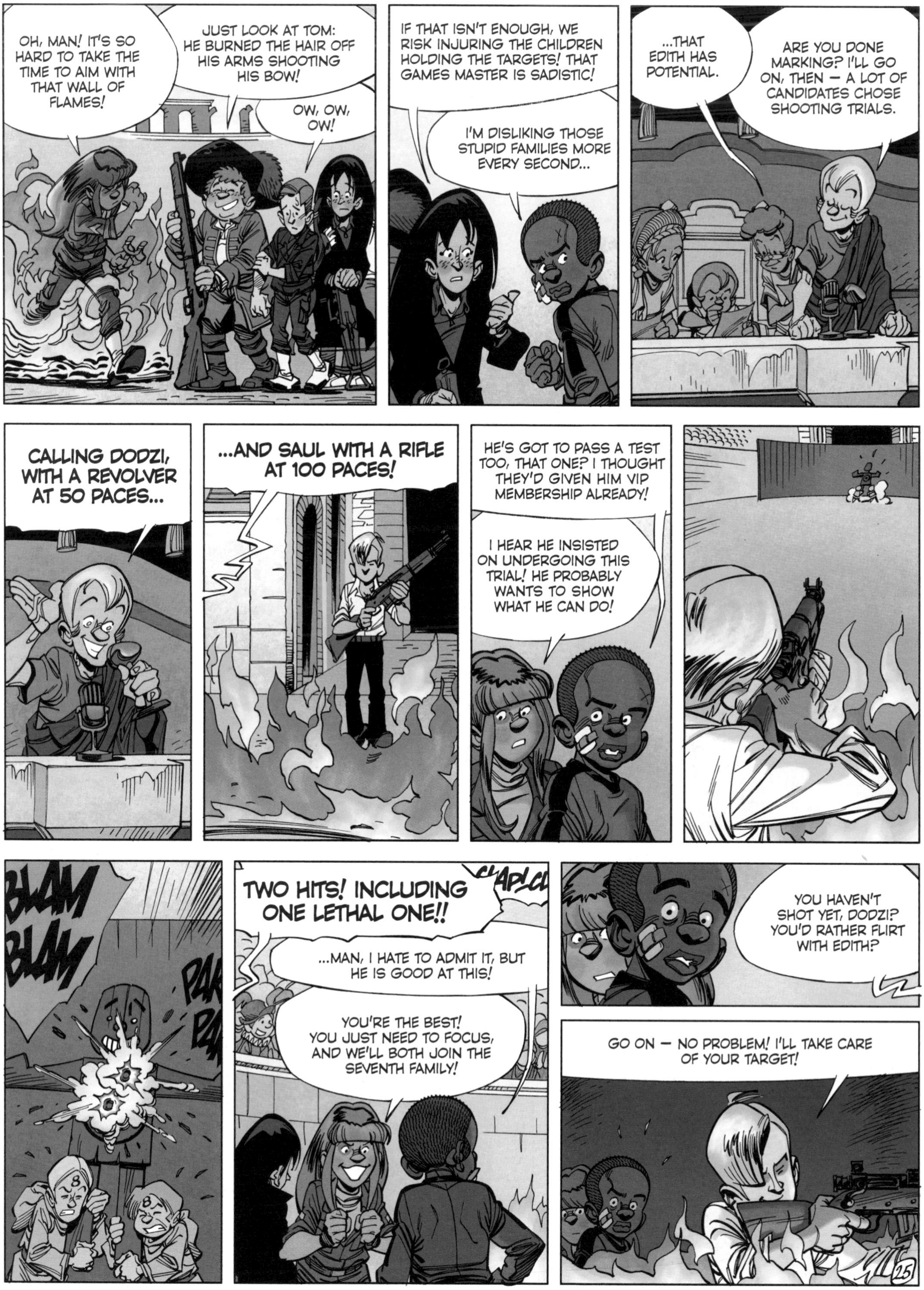
OH, MAN! IT'S SO HARD TO TAKE THE TIME TO AIM WITH THAT WALL OF FLAMES!
JUST LOOK AT TOM: HE BURNED THE HAIR OFF HIS ARMS SHOOTING HIS BOW!
OW, OW, OW!
IF THAT ISN'T ENOUGH, WE RISK INJURING THE CHILDREN HOLDING THE TARGETS! THAT GAMES MASTER IS SADISTIC!
I'M DISLIKING THOSE STUPID FAMILIES MORE EVERY SECOND...
...THAT EDITH HAS POTENTIAL.
ARE YOU DONE MARKING? I'LL GO ON, THEN — A LOT OF CANDIDATES CHOSE SHOOTING TRIALS.
CALLING DODZI, WITH A REVOLVER AT 50 PACES...
...AND SAUL WITH A RIFLE AT 100 PACES!
HE'S GOT TO PASS A TEST TOO, THAT ONE? I THOUGHT THEY'D GIVEN HIM VIP MEMBERSHIP ALREADY!
I HEAR HE INSISTED ON UNDERGOING THIS TRIAL! HE PROBABLY WANTS TO SHOW WHAT HE CAN DO!
BLAM
BLAM
TWO HITS! INCLUDING ONE LETHAL ONE!!
...MAN, I HATE TO ADMIT IT, BUT HE IS GOOD AT THIS!
YOU'RE THE BEST! YOU JUST NEED TO FOCUS, AND WE'LL BOTH JOIN THE SEVENTH FAMILY!
YOU HAVEN'T SHOT YET, DODZI? YOU'D RATHER FLIRT WITH EDITH?
GO ON — NO PROBLEM! I'LL TAKE CARE OF YOUR TARGET!

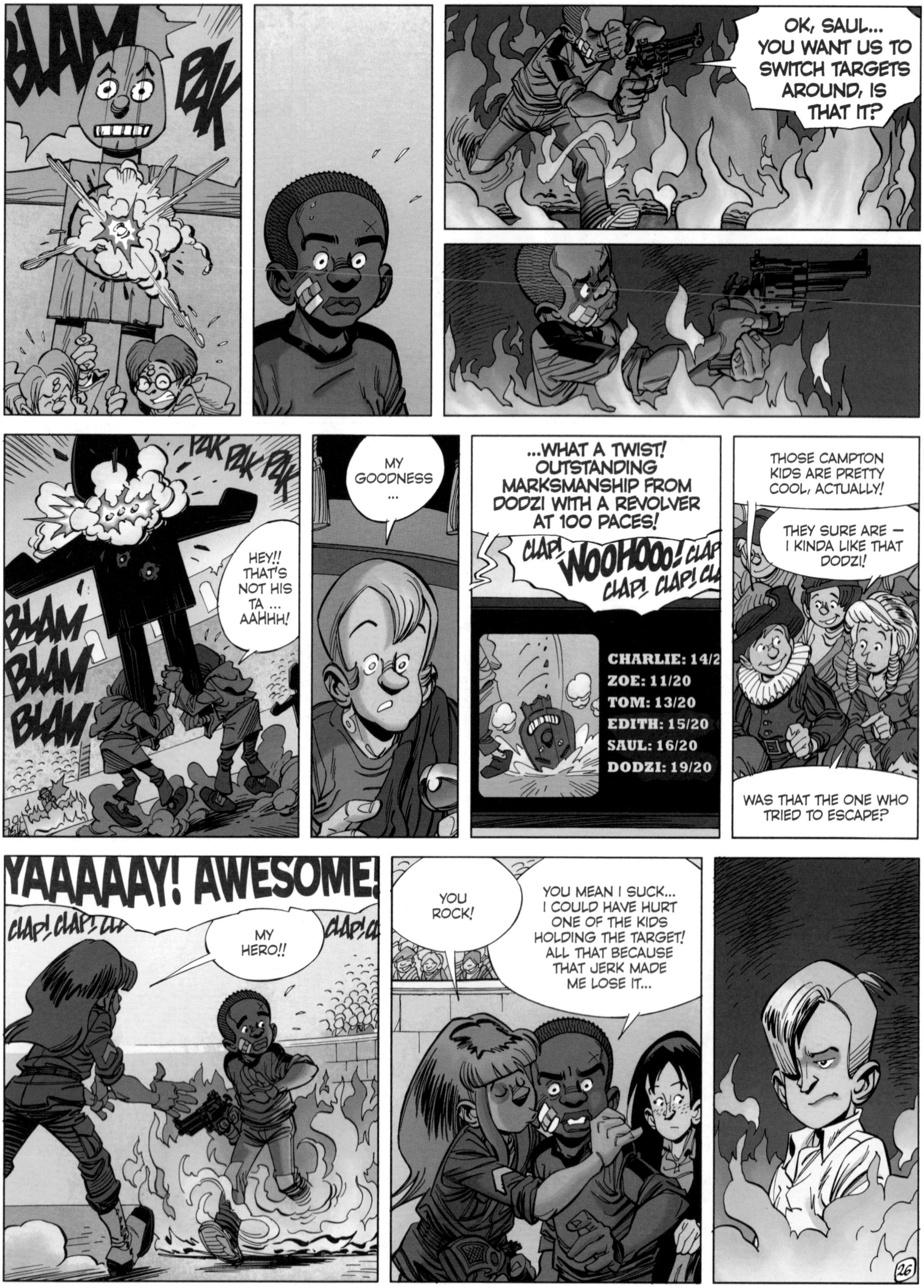
BLAM
PAK
OK, SAUL... YOU WANT US TO SWITCH TARGETS AROUND, IS THAT IT?
PAK PAK PAK
BLAM BLAM BLAM
HEY!! THAT'S NOT HIS TA ... AAHHH!
MY GOODNESS ...
...WHAT A TWIST! OUTSTANDING MARKSMANSHIP FROM DODZI WITH A REVOLVER AT 100 PACES!
CLAP! WOOHOOO! CLAP! CLAP! CLAP!
CHARLIE: 14/2
ZOE: 11/20
TOM: 13/20
EDITH: 15/20
SAUL: 16/20
DODZI: 19/20
THOSE CAMPTON KIDS ARE PRETTY COOL, ACTUALLY!
THEY SURE ARE — I KINDA LIKE THAT DODZI!
WAS THAT THE ONE WHO TRIED TO ESCAPE?
YAAAAAY! AWESOME!
CLAP! CLAP!
CLAP!
MY HERO!!
YOU ROCK!
YOU MEAN I SUCK... I COULD HAVE HURT ONE OF THE KIDS HOLDING THE TARGET! ALL THAT BECAUSE THAT JERK MADE ME LOSE IT...
26

THE HAND OF ALDERIC ISN'T REACTING...

LEILA'S NOT REMEMBERING HER DEATH, EITHER, SO NO CLUES TO BE GLEANED FROM THAT QUARTER.

PERHAPS A SLIGHT SHOCK WILL FORCE HIDDEN EMOTIONS BACK TO THE SURFACE.

THIS WAY, LEILA...

THIS IS THE WHITE CHAMBER.

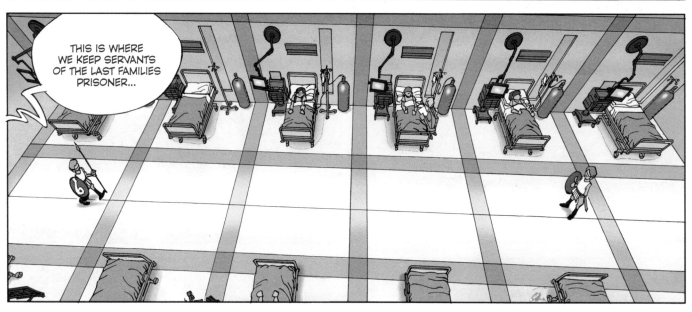

THIS IS WHERE WE KEEP SERVANTS OF THE LAST FAMILIES PRISONER...

...AND WHERE YOUR FRIEND BORIS WILL REMAIN FOR EVER, SLEEPING A DREAMLESS SLEEP ... SO THAT HE MAY NEVER AGAIN BE A THREAT.

AN ETERNITY SPENT IN NOTHINGNESS! THAT'S THE FATE IN STORE FOR YOU IF YOU CONTINUE LYING TO US!!

I'M NOT LYING! I... I JUST DON'T REMEMBER ANYTHING!!

OR MAYBE YOU SIMPLY REFUSE TO FACE THE TRUTH.

REMEMBER HOW YOU DIED, LEILA!

...I DON'T...

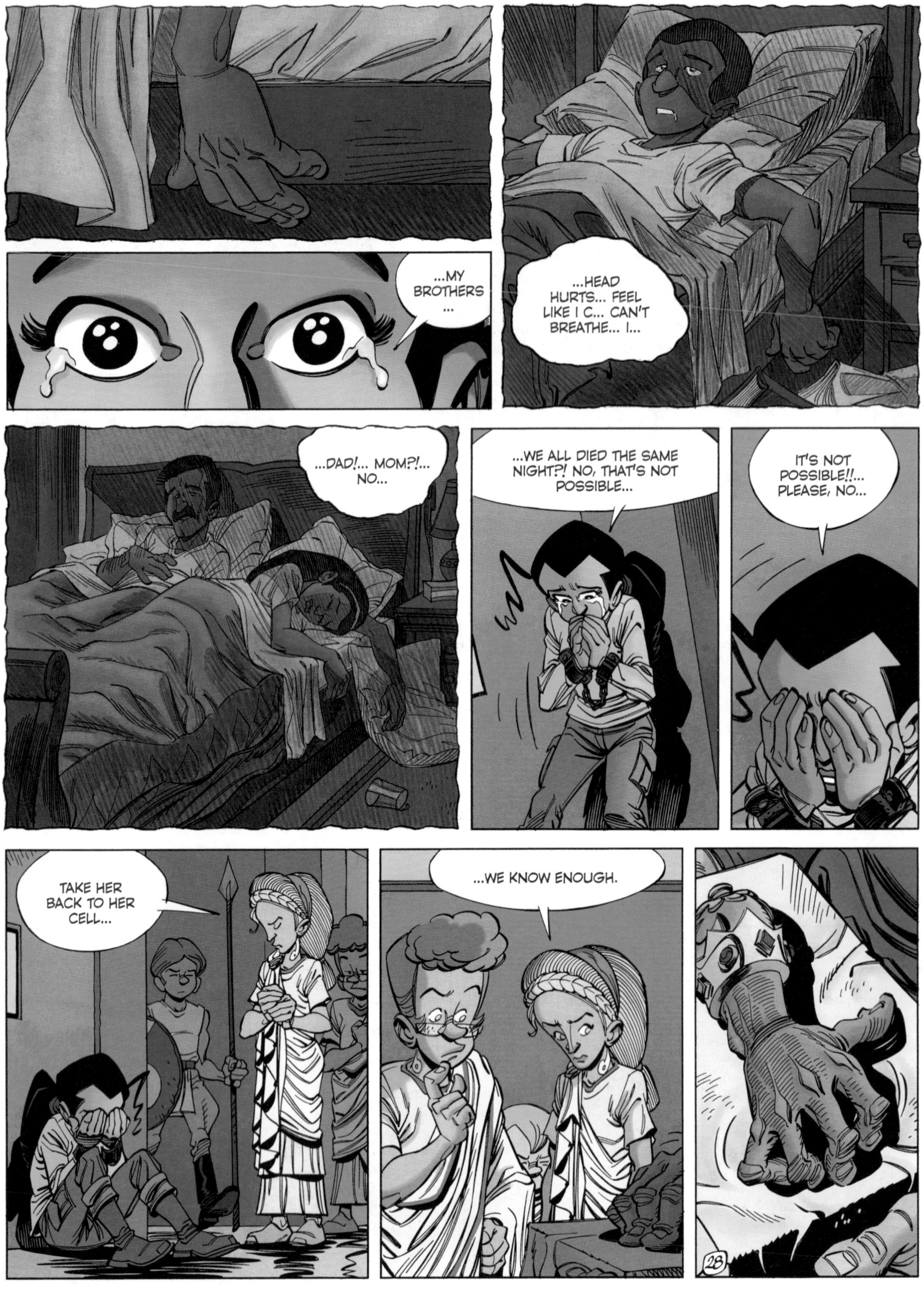
...MY BROTHERS ...
...HEAD HURTS... FEEL LIKE I C... CAN'T BREATHE... I...
...DAD!... MOM?!... NO...
...WE ALL DIED THE SAME NIGHT?! NO, THAT'S NOT POSSIBLE...
IT'S NOT POSSIBLE!!... PLEASE, NO...
TAKE HER BACK TO HER CELL...
...WE KNOW ENOUGH.
28

ONLY A FEW SECONDS LEFT, MILA...

DONE!! X=125 AND Y=20!

CORRRRECT ANSWER!!

I NOW YIELD THE STAGE TO ANTON, WHO ELECTED TO GIVE A PRESENTATION ON A TOPIC OF HIS CHOICE...

...A PRESENTATION I INVITE YOU TO DISRUPT SLIGHTLY, DEAR SPECTATORS, USING THE STONES YOU WILL FIND AT YOUR FEET!

YEAAAAAAH!

THANK YOU... I WOULD LIKE TO SHARE WITH YOU...

WE DON'T CAAAARE!

TRY TO DODGE THIS INSTEAD!!

AAAH!

PAK

PAK

PAK

PAK

PAK

...SHARE WITH YOU MY LATEST THEORIES ON WHAT I WILL CALL 'BETWEENOLOGY' — OR THE STUDY OF THE IN-BETWEEN WORLD!!

PAK PAK

PAK

PAK

WHAT?

STUDY OF THE IN-BETWEEN WORLD?

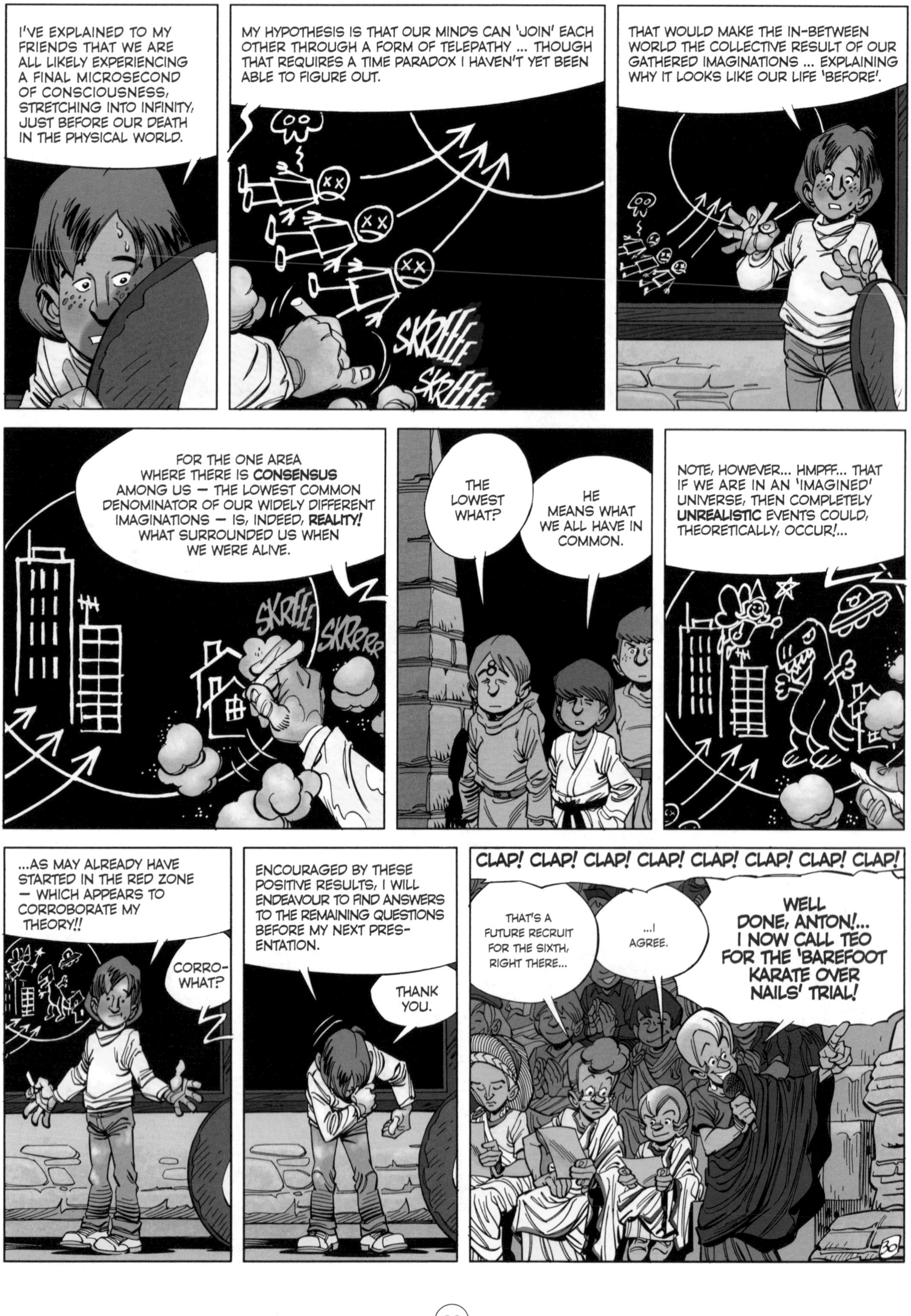
I'VE EXPLAINED TO MY FRIENDS THAT WE ARE ALL LIKELY EXPERIENCING A FINAL MICROSECOND OF CONSCIOUSNESS, STRETCHING INTO INFINITY, JUST BEFORE OUR DEATH IN THE PHYSICAL WORLD.
MY HYPOTHESIS IS THAT OUR MINDS CAN 'JOIN' EACH OTHER THROUGH A FORM OF TELEPATHY ... THOUGH THAT REQUIRES A TIME PARADOX I HAVEN'T YET BEEN ABLE TO FIGURE OUT.
SKREEEE
SKREEEE
THAT WOULD MAKE THE IN-BETWEEN WORLD THE COLLECTIVE RESULT OF OUR GATHERED IMAGINATIONS ... EXPLAINING WHY IT LOOKS LIKE OUR LIFE 'BEFORE'.
FOR THE ONE AREA WHERE THERE IS **CONSENSUS** AMONG US — THE LOWEST COMMON DENOMINATOR OF OUR WIDELY DIFFERENT IMAGINATIONS — IS, INDEED, **REALITY!** WHAT SURROUNDED US WHEN WE WERE ALIVE.
SKREEE
SKRRRR
THE LOWEST WHAT?
HE MEANS WHAT WE ALL HAVE IN COMMON.
NOTE, HOWEVER... HMPFF... THAT IF WE ARE IN AN 'IMAGINED' UNIVERSE, THEN COMPLETELY **UNREALISTIC** EVENTS COULD, THEORETICALLY, OCCUR!...
...AS MAY ALREADY HAVE STARTED IN THE RED ZONE — WHICH APPEARS TO CORROBORATE MY THEORY!!
CORRO-WHAT?
ENCOURAGED BY THESE POSITIVE RESULTS, I WILL ENDEAVOUR TO FIND ANSWERS TO THE REMAINING QUESTIONS BEFORE MY NEXT PRES-ENTATION.
THANK YOU.
CLAP! CLAP! CLAP! CLAP! CLAP! CLAP! CLAP! CLAP!
THAT'S A FUTURE RECRUIT FOR THE SIXTH, RIGHT THERE...
...I AGREE.
WELL DONE, ANTON!... I NOW CALL TEO FOR THE 'BAREFOOT KARATE OVER NAILS' TRIAL!
30

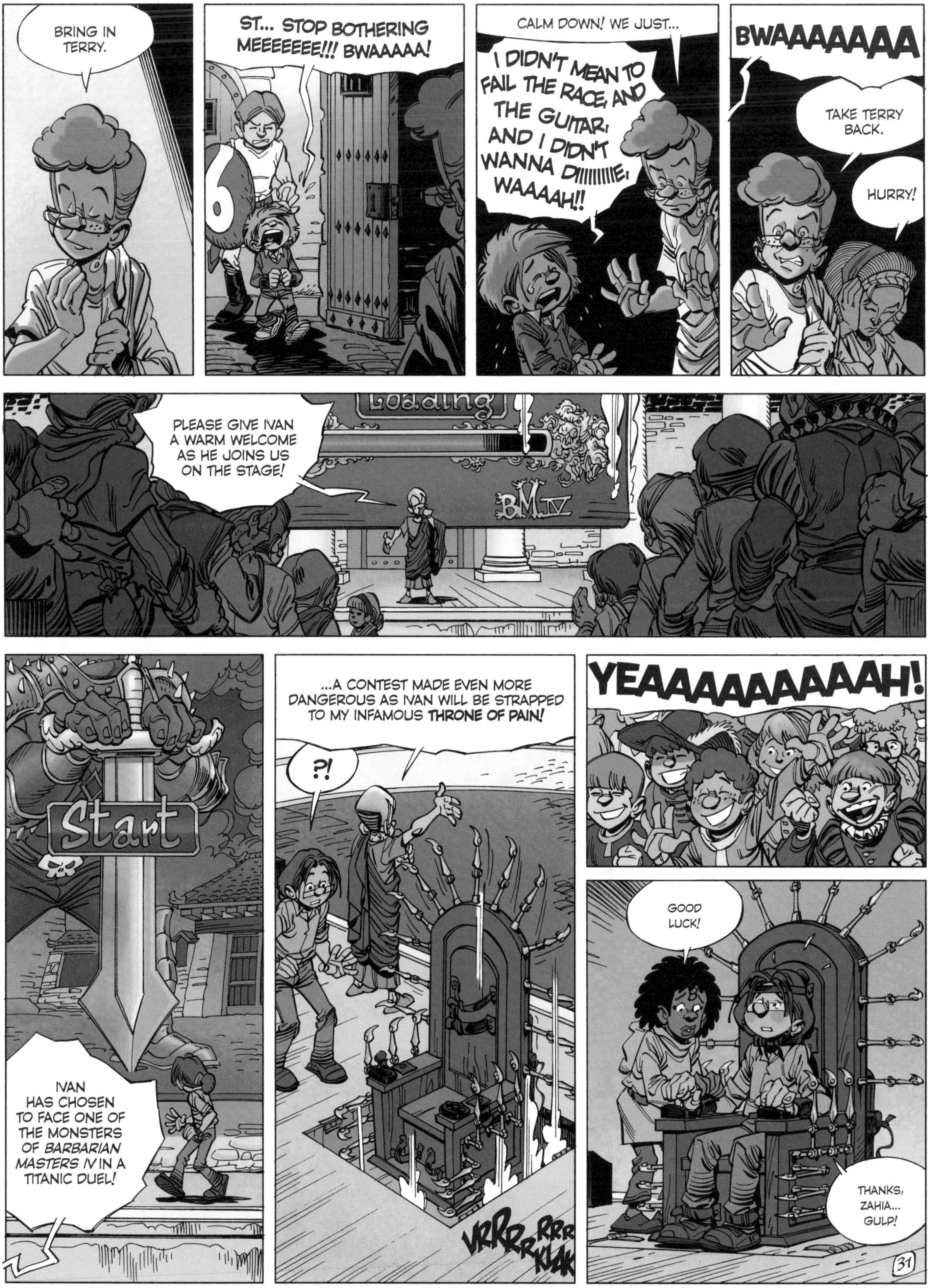
BRING IN TERRY.
ST... STOP BOTHERING MEEEEEEE!!! BWAAAAA!
CALM DOWN! WE JUST...
I DIDN'T MEAN TO FAIL THE RACE, AND THE GUITAR, AND I DIDN'T WANNA DIIIIIIIIE, WAAAAH!!
BWAAAAAAA
TAKE TERRY BACK.
HURRY!
PLEASE GIVE IVAN A WARM WELCOME AS HE JOINS US ON THE STAGE!
Loading
B.M.IV
Start
IVAN HAS CHOSEN TO FACE ONE OF THE MONSTERS OF *BARBARIAN MASTERS IV* IN A TITANIC DUEL!
...A CONTEST MADE EVEN MORE DANGEROUS AS IVAN WILL BE STRAPPED TO MY INFAMOUS **THRONE OF PAIN!**
?!
VRRRRRRR KLAK
YEAAAAAAAAAH!
GOOD LUCK!
THANKS, ZAHIA... GULP!
31

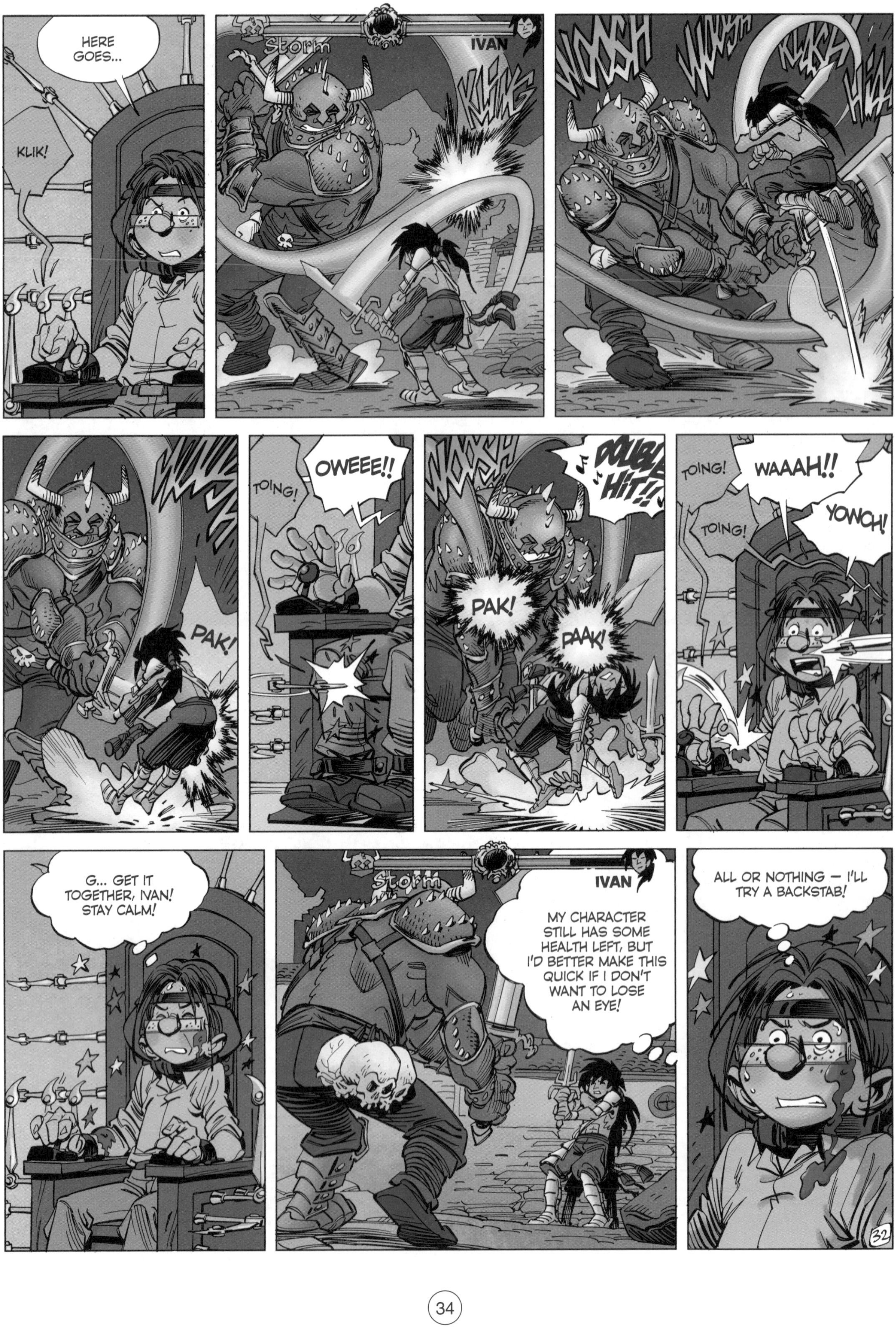
HERE GOES...
KLIK!
Storm
IVAN
KLING
WOOSH
WOOSH
KLACK
HIA
WOOSH
PAK!
TOING!
OWEEE!!
WOOSH
DOUBLE HIT!!
PAK!
PAAK!
TOING!
WAAAH!!
TOING!
YONCH!
G... GET IT TOGETHER, IVAN! STAY CALM!
Storm
IVAN
MY CHARACTER STILL HAS SOME HEALTH LEFT, BUT I'D BETTER MAKE THIS QUICK IF I DON'T WANT TO LOSE AN EYE!
ALL OR NOTHING — I'LL TRY A BACKSTAB!
32

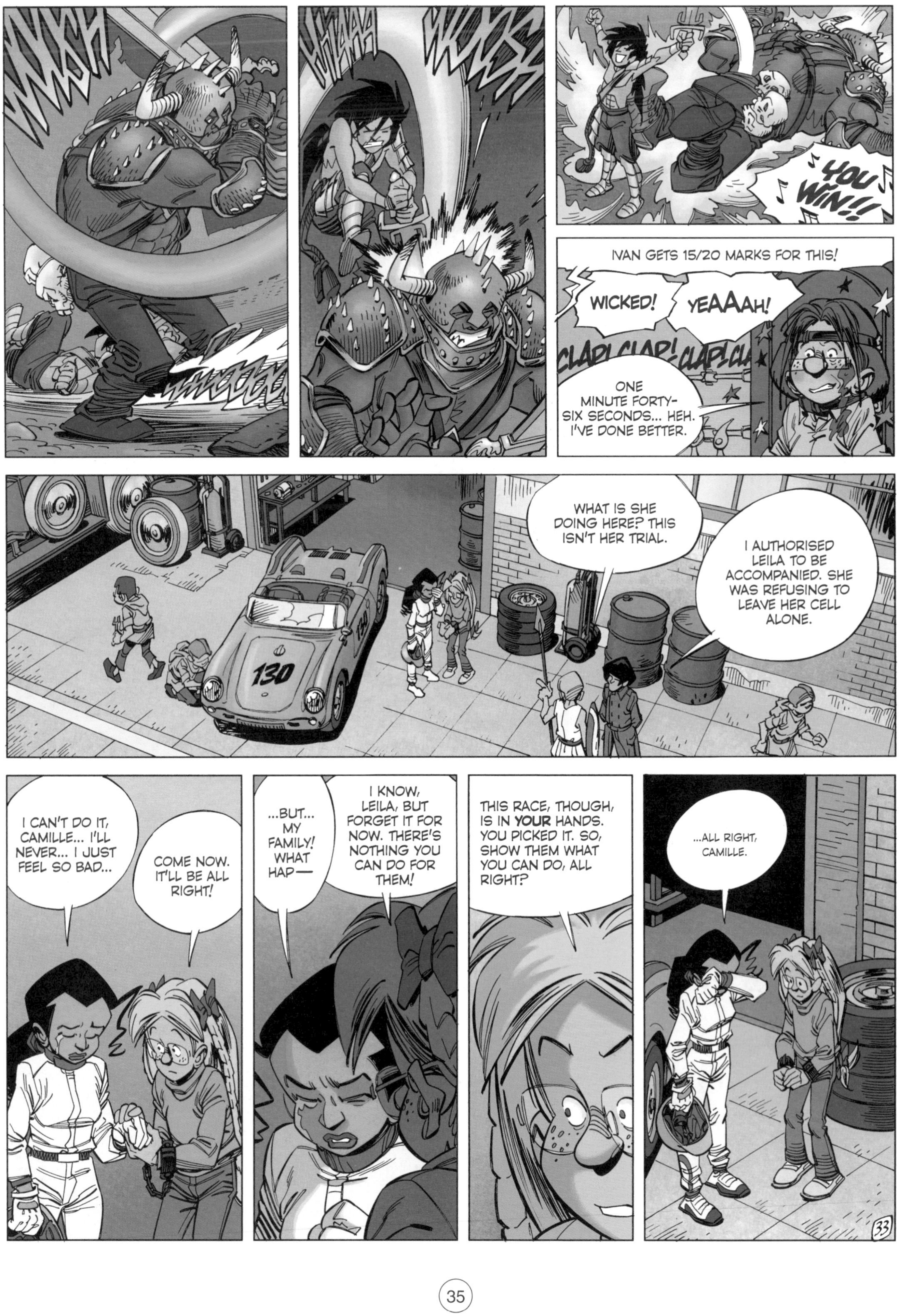
WISH
WHAAA
WUSH
YOU WIN!!
IVAN GETS 15/20 MARKS FOR THIS!
WICKED!
YEAAAH!
CLAP! CLAP! CLAP! CLA
ONE MINUTE FORTY-SIX SECONDS... HEH. I'VE DONE BETTER.
WHAT IS SHE DOING HERE? THIS ISN'T HER TRIAL.
I AUTHORISED LEILA TO BE ACCOMPANIED. SHE WAS REFUSING TO LEAVE HER CELL ALONE.
130
I CAN'T DO IT, CAMILLE... I'LL NEVER... I JUST FEEL SO BAD...
COME NOW. IT'LL BE ALL RIGHT!
...BUT... MY FAMILY! WHAT HAP—
I KNOW, LEILA, BUT FORGET IT FOR NOW. THERE'S NOTHING YOU CAN DO FOR THEM!
THIS RACE, THOUGH, IS IN **YOUR** HANDS. YOU PICKED IT. SO, SHOW THEM WHAT YOU CAN DO, ALL RIGHT?
...ALL RIGHT, CAMILLE.
33

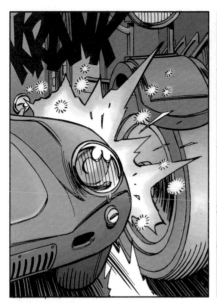

AND AS THE TWO VEHICLES ZOOM THROUGH THE STREETS OF NEOSALEM, DEAR SPECTATORS!...

...WILL LEILA MANAGE TO OVERTAKE CRAFTY ACHILLES — WITHOUT HARMING ANY INNOCENTS ALONG THE WAY?

AAAAH!

WHAT?!

WHOAAAAAA!

OH DEAR, THIS RACE IS EXTREMELY DANGEROUS!

YES, SOME OF THE ADMISSION TRIALS ARE PRETTY TOUGH!

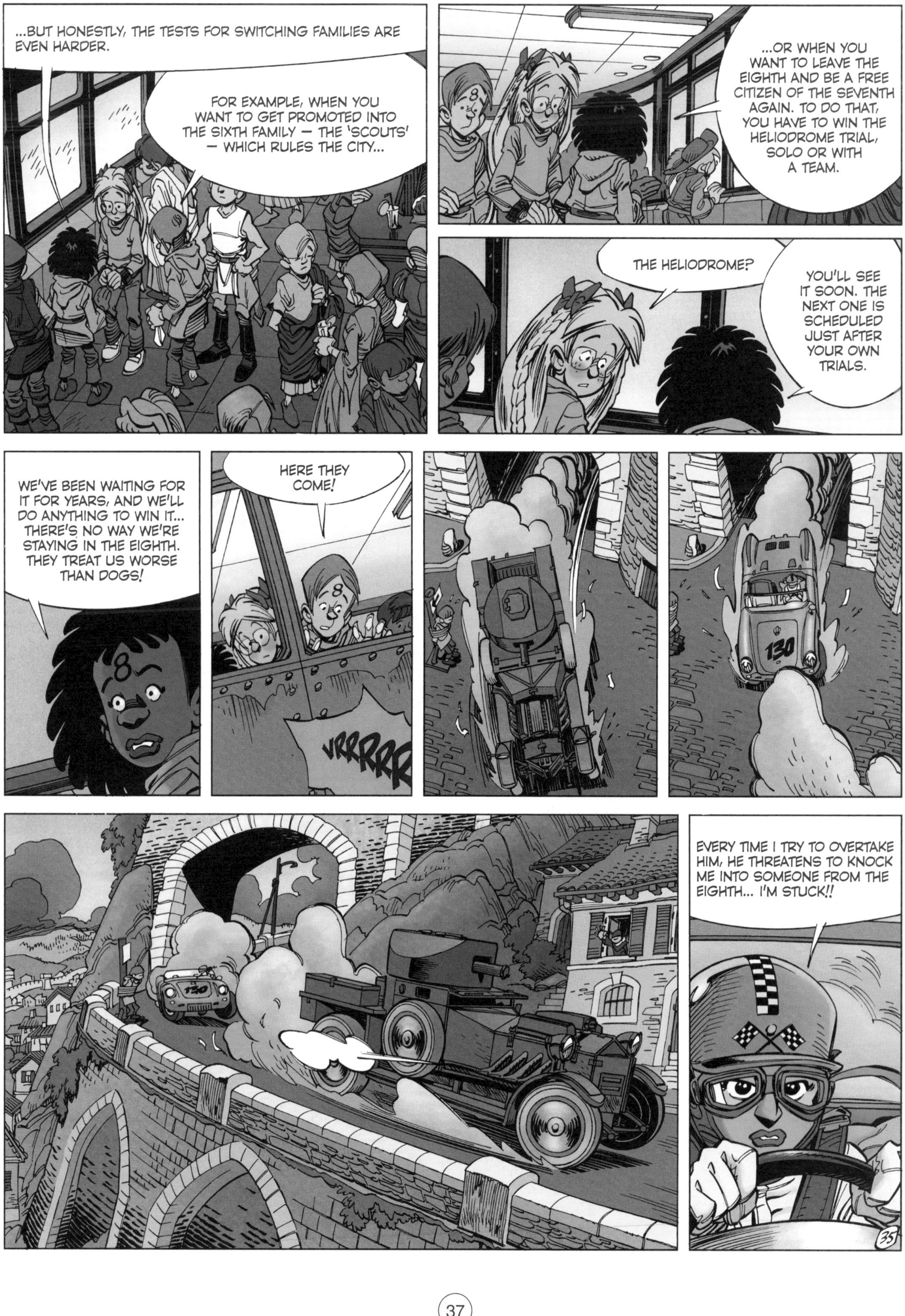
...BUT HONESTLY, THE TESTS FOR SWITCHING FAMILIES ARE EVEN HARDER.
FOR EXAMPLE, WHEN YOU WANT TO GET PROMOTED INTO THE SIXTH FAMILY — THE 'SCOUTS' — WHICH RULES THE CITY...
...OR WHEN YOU WANT TO LEAVE THE EIGHTH AND BE A FREE CITIZEN OF THE SEVENTH AGAIN. TO DO THAT, YOU HAVE TO WIN THE HELIODROME TRIAL, SOLO OR WITH A TEAM.
THE HELIODROME?
YOU'LL SEE IT SOON. THE NEXT ONE IS SCHEDULED JUST AFTER YOUR OWN TRIALS.
WE'VE BEEN WAITING FOR IT FOR YEARS, AND WE'LL DO ANYTHING TO WIN IT... THERE'S NO WAY WE'RE STAYING IN THE EIGHTH. THEY TREAT US WORSE THAN DOGS!
HERE THEY COME!
VRRRRRR
EVERY TIME I TRY TO OVERTAKE HIM, HE THREATENS TO KNOCK ME INTO SOMEONE FROM THE EIGHTH... I'M STUCK!!
35

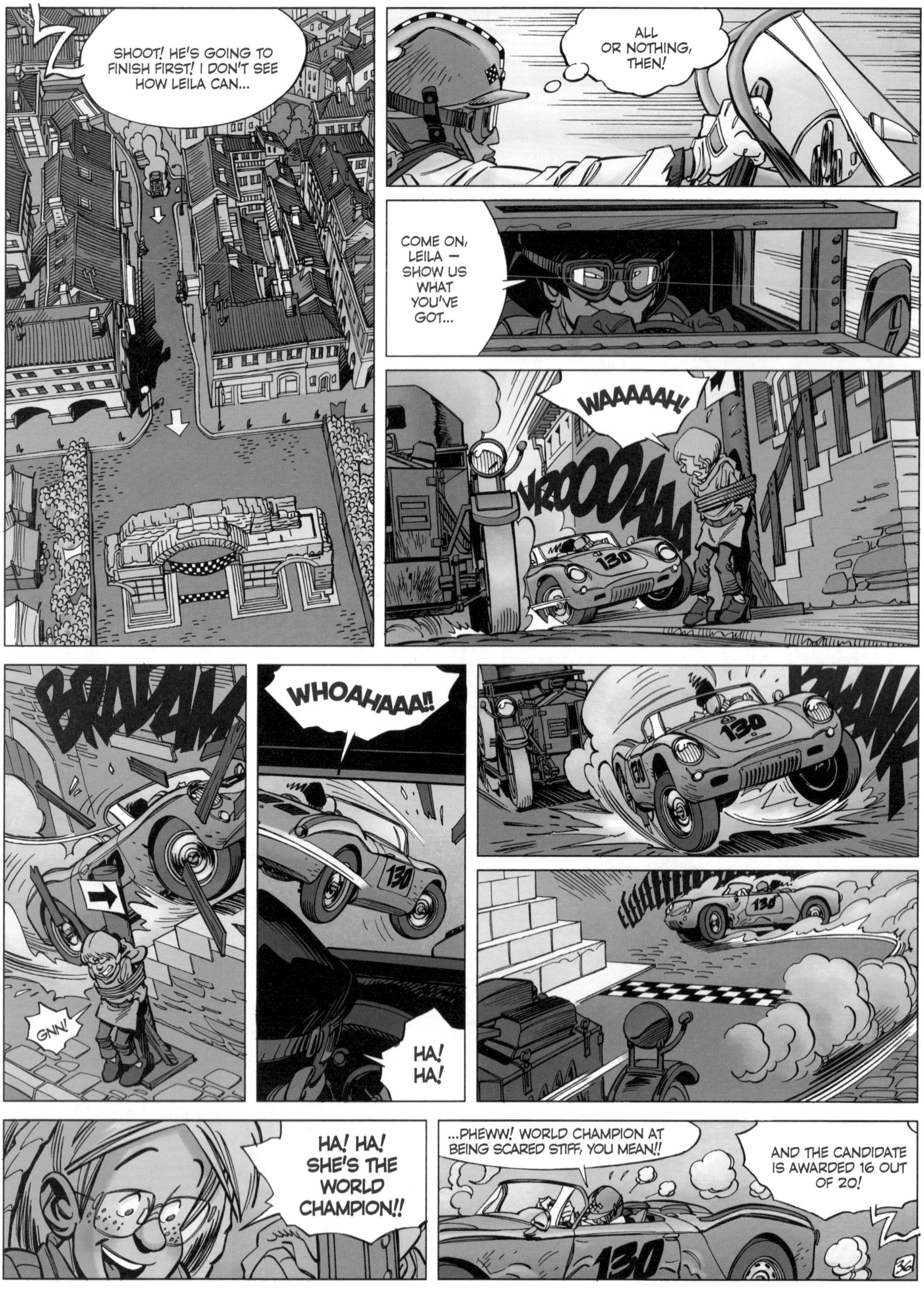
SHOOT! HE'S GOING TO FINISH FIRST! I DON'T SEE HOW LEILA CAN...
ALL OR NOTHING, THEN!
COME ON, LEILA — SHOW US WHAT YOU'VE GOT...
WAAAAAH!
VROOOAAAA
BRAAAM
WHOAHAAA!!
HA! HA!
GNN!
ELLLLLLLLL
HA! HA! SHE'S THE WORLD CHAMPION!!
...PHEWW! WORLD CHAMPION AT BEING SCARED STIFF, YOU MEAN!!
AND THE CANDIDATE IS AWARDED 16 OUT OF 20!

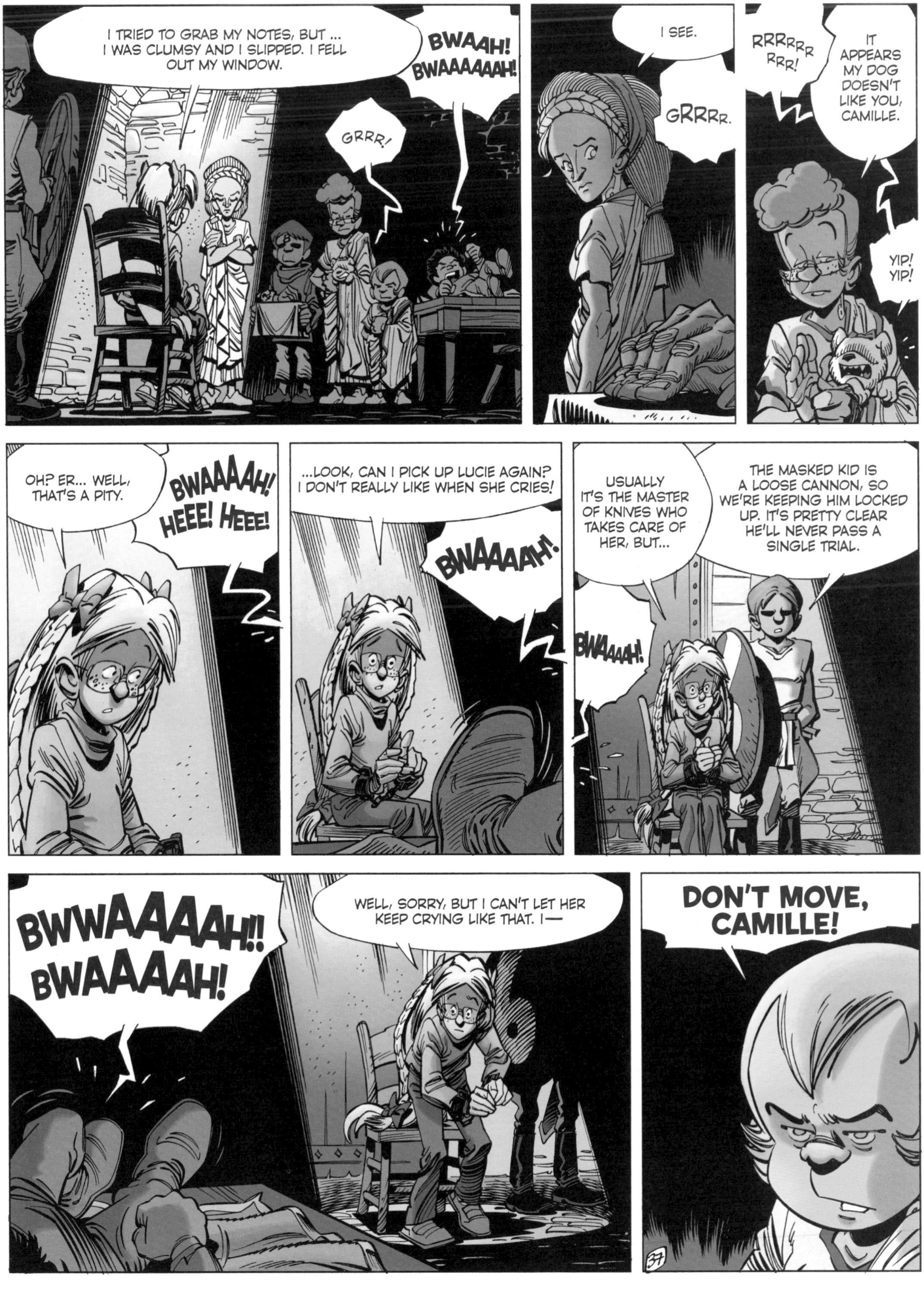
I TRIED TO GRAB MY NOTES, BUT ... I WAS CLUMSY AND I SLIPPED. I FELL OUT MY WINDOW.
BWAAH! BWAAAAAAH!
GRRR!
I SEE.
GRRRR.
RRRRRRR RRR!
IT APPEARS MY DOG DOESN'T LIKE YOU, CAMILLE.
YIP! YIP!
OH? ER... WELL, THAT'S A PITY.
BWAAAAH! HEEE! HEEE!
...LOOK, CAN I PICK UP LUCIE AGAIN? I DON'T REALLY LIKE WHEN SHE CRIES!
BWAAAAH!
USUALLY IT'S THE MASTER OF KNIVES WHO TAKES CARE OF HER, BUT...
THE MASKED KID IS A LOOSE CANNON, SO WE'RE KEEPING HIM LOCKED UP. IT'S PRETTY CLEAR HE'LL NEVER PASS A SINGLE TRIAL.
BWAAAAH!
BWWAAAAAH!! BWAAAAH!
WELL, SORRY, BUT I CAN'T LET HER KEEP CRYING LIKE THAT. I—
DON'T MOVE, CAMILLE!
37

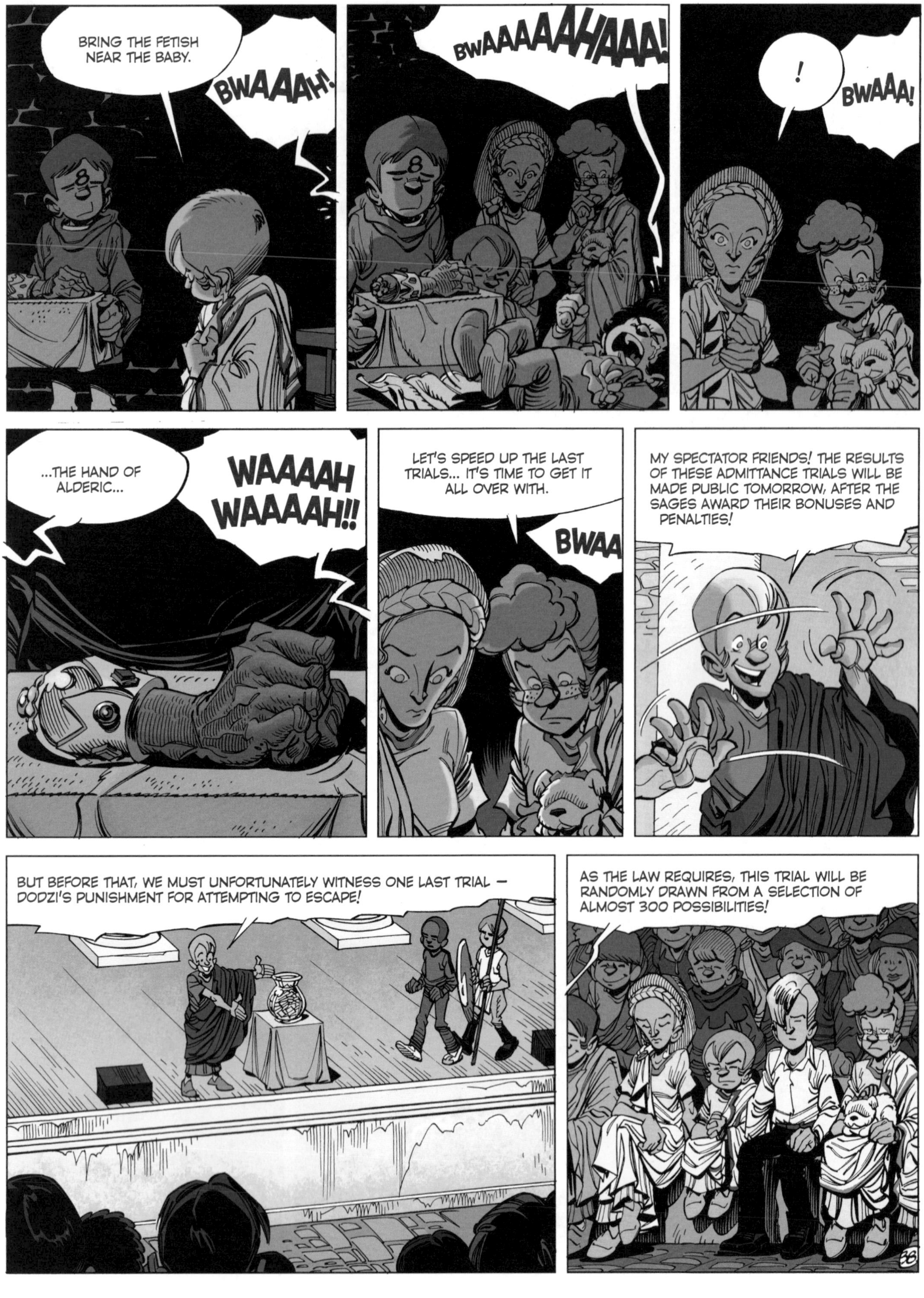
BRING THE FETISH NEAR THE BABY.
BWAAAH!
BWAAAAAAHAAA!
!
BWAAA!
...THE HAND OF ALDERIC...
WAAAAH WAAAAH!!
LET'S SPEED UP THE LAST TRIALS... IT'S TIME TO GET IT ALL OVER WITH.
BWAA
MY SPECTATOR FRIENDS! THE RESULTS OF THESE ADMITTANCE TRIALS WILL BE MADE PUBLIC TOMORROW, AFTER THE SAGES AWARD THEIR BONUSES AND PENALTIES!
BUT BEFORE THAT, WE MUST UNFORTUNATELY WITNESS ONE LAST TRIAL — DODZI'S PUNISHMENT FOR ATTEMPTING TO ESCAPE!
AS THE LAW REQUIRES, THIS TRIAL WILL BE RANDOMLY DRAWN FROM A SELECTION OF ALMOST 300 POSSIBILITIES!

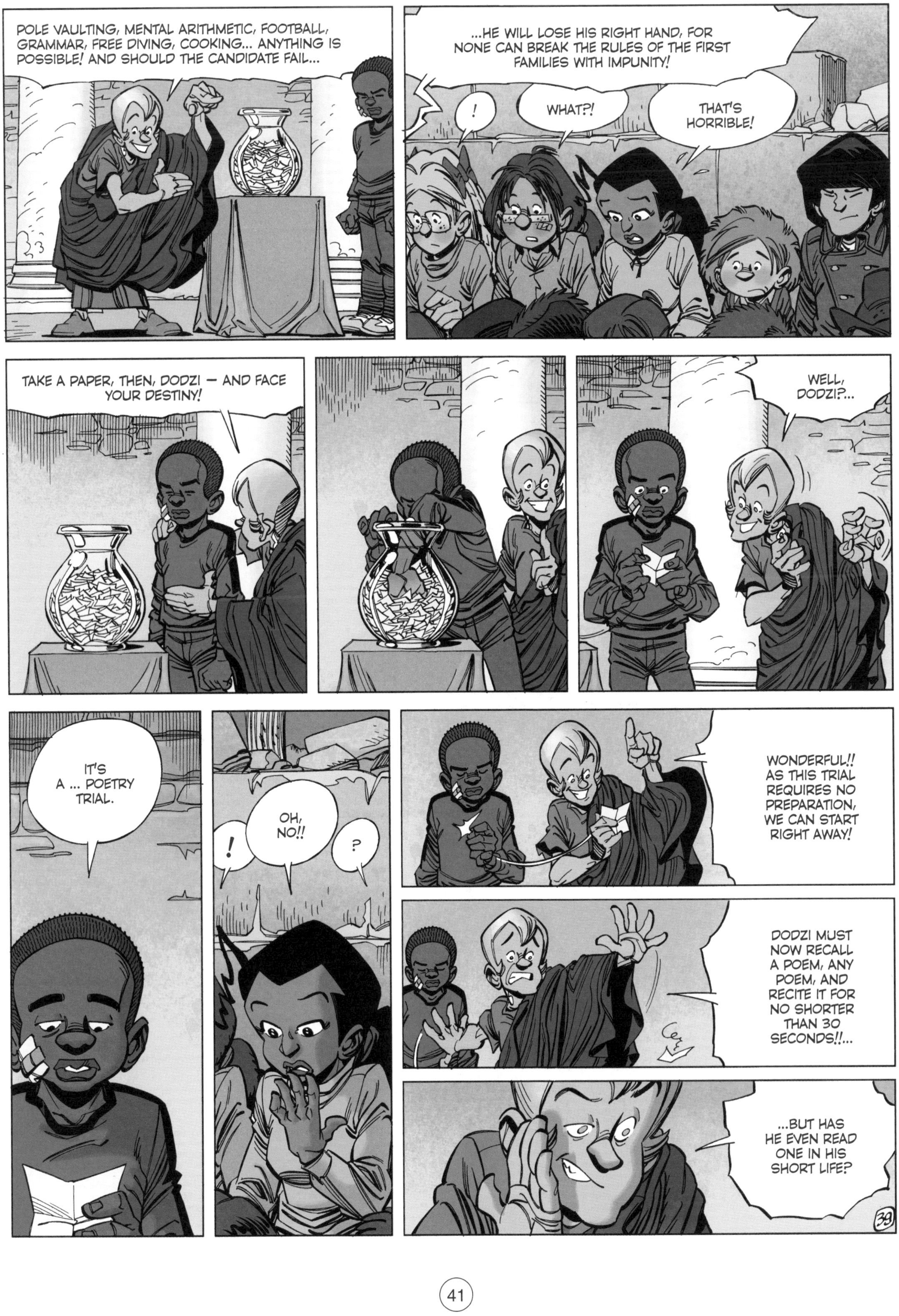
POLE VAULTING, MENTAL ARITHMETIC, FOOTBALL, GRAMMAR, FREE DIVING, COOKING... ANYTHING IS POSSIBLE! AND SHOULD THE CANDIDATE FAIL...
...HE WILL LOSE HIS RIGHT HAND, FOR NONE CAN BREAK THE RULES OF THE FIRST FAMILIES WITH IMPUNITY!
!
WHAT?!
THAT'S HORRIBLE!
TAKE A PAPER, THEN, DODZI — AND FACE YOUR DESTINY!
WELL, DODZI?...
IT'S A ... POETRY TRIAL.
!
OH, NO!!
?
WONDERFUL!! AS THIS TRIAL REQUIRES NO PREPARATION, WE CAN START RIGHT AWAY!
DODZI MUST NOW RECALL A POEM, ANY POEM, AND RECITE IT FOR NO SHORTER THAN 30 SECONDS!!...
...BUT HAS HE EVEN READ ONE IN HIS SHORT LIFE?

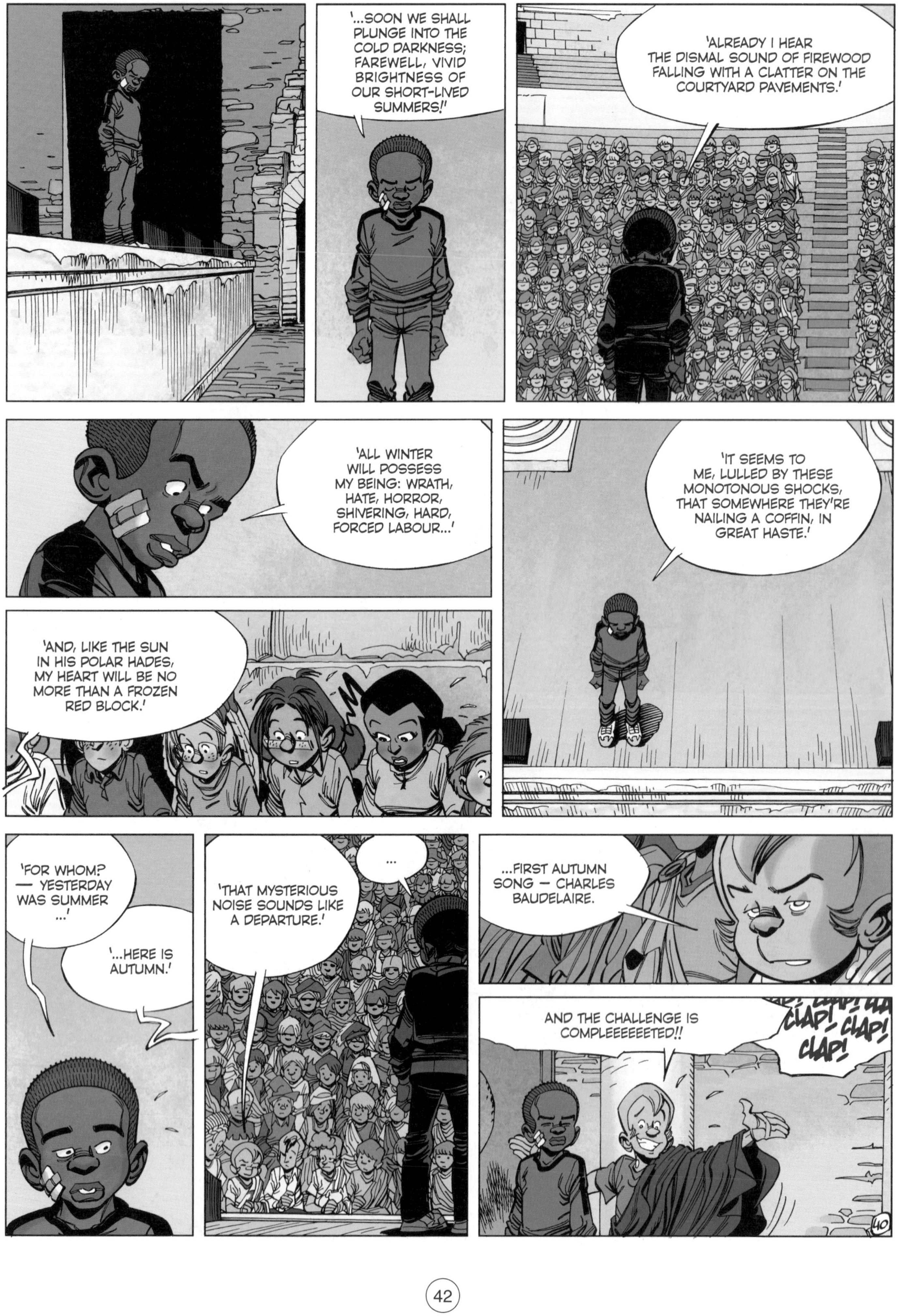
'...SOON WE SHALL PLUNGE INTO THE COLD DARKNESS; FAREWELL, VIVID BRIGHTNESS OF OUR SHORT-LIVED SUMMERS!'
'ALREADY I HEAR THE DISMAL SOUND OF FIREWOOD FALLING WITH A CLATTER ON THE COURTYARD PAVEMENTS.'
'ALL WINTER WILL POSSESS MY BEING: WRATH, HATE, HORROR, SHIVERING, HARD, FORCED LABOUR...'
'IT SEEMS TO ME, LULLED BY THESE MONOTONOUS SHOCKS, THAT SOMEWHERE THEY'RE NAILING A COFFIN, IN GREAT HASTE.'
'AND, LIKE THE SUN IN HIS POLAR HADES, MY HEART WILL BE NO MORE THAN A FROZEN RED BLOCK.'
'FOR WHOM? — YESTERDAY WAS SUMMER ...'
'...HERE IS AUTUMN.'
'THAT MYSTERIOUS NOISE SOUNDS LIKE A DEPARTURE.'
...
...FIRST AUTUMN SONG — CHARLES BAUDELAIRE.
AND THE CHALLENGE IS COMPLEEEEEETED!!
CLAP! CLAP! CLAP! CLAP!
40

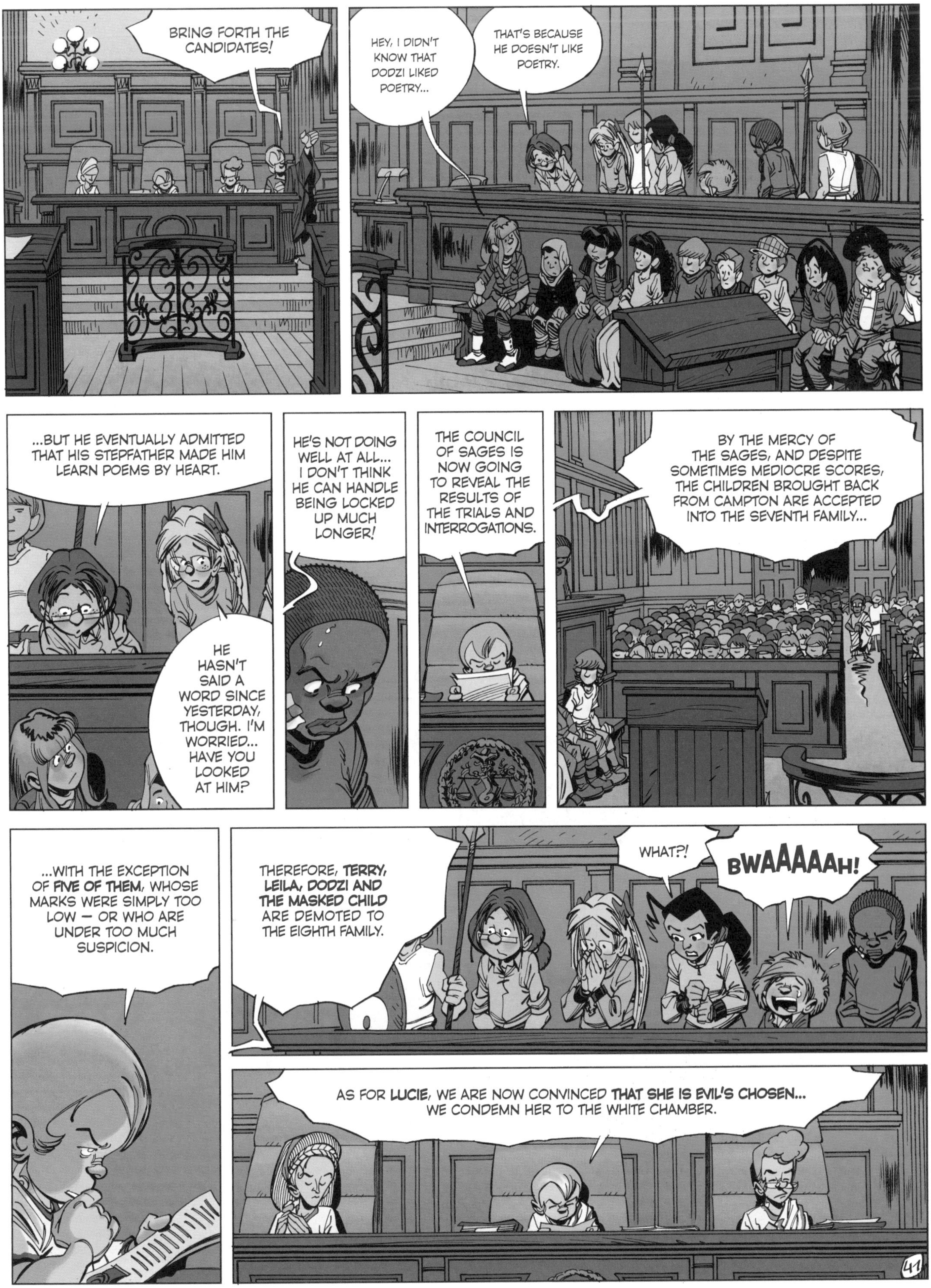
BRING FORTH THE CANDIDATES!
HEY, I DIDN'T KNOW THAT DODZI LIKED POETRY...
THAT'S BECAUSE HE DOESN'T LIKE POETRY.
...BUT HE EVENTUALLY ADMITTED THAT HIS STEPFATHER MADE HIM LEARN POEMS BY HEART.
HE HASN'T SAID A WORD SINCE YESTERDAY, THOUGH. I'M WORRIED... HAVE YOU LOOKED AT HIM?
HE'S NOT DOING WELL AT ALL... I DON'T THINK HE CAN HANDLE BEING LOCKED UP MUCH LONGER!
THE COUNCIL OF SAGES IS NOW GOING TO REVEAL THE RESULTS OF THE TRIALS AND INTERROGATIONS.
BY THE MERCY OF THE SAGES, AND DESPITE SOMETIMES MEDIOCRE SCORES, THE CHILDREN BROUGHT BACK FROM CAMPTON ARE ACCEPTED INTO THE SEVENTH FAMILY...
...WITH THE EXCEPTION OF **FIVE OF THEM**, WHOSE MARKS WERE SIMPLY TOO LOW — OR WHO ARE UNDER TOO MUCH SUSPICION.
THEREFORE, **TERRY, LEILA, DODZI AND THE MASKED CHILD** ARE DEMOTED TO THE EIGHTH FAMILY.
WHAT?!
BWAAAAAH!
AS FOR **LUCIE**, WE ARE NOW CONVINCED **THAT SHE IS EVIL'S CHOSEN...** WE CONDEMN HER TO THE WHITE CHAMBER.
41

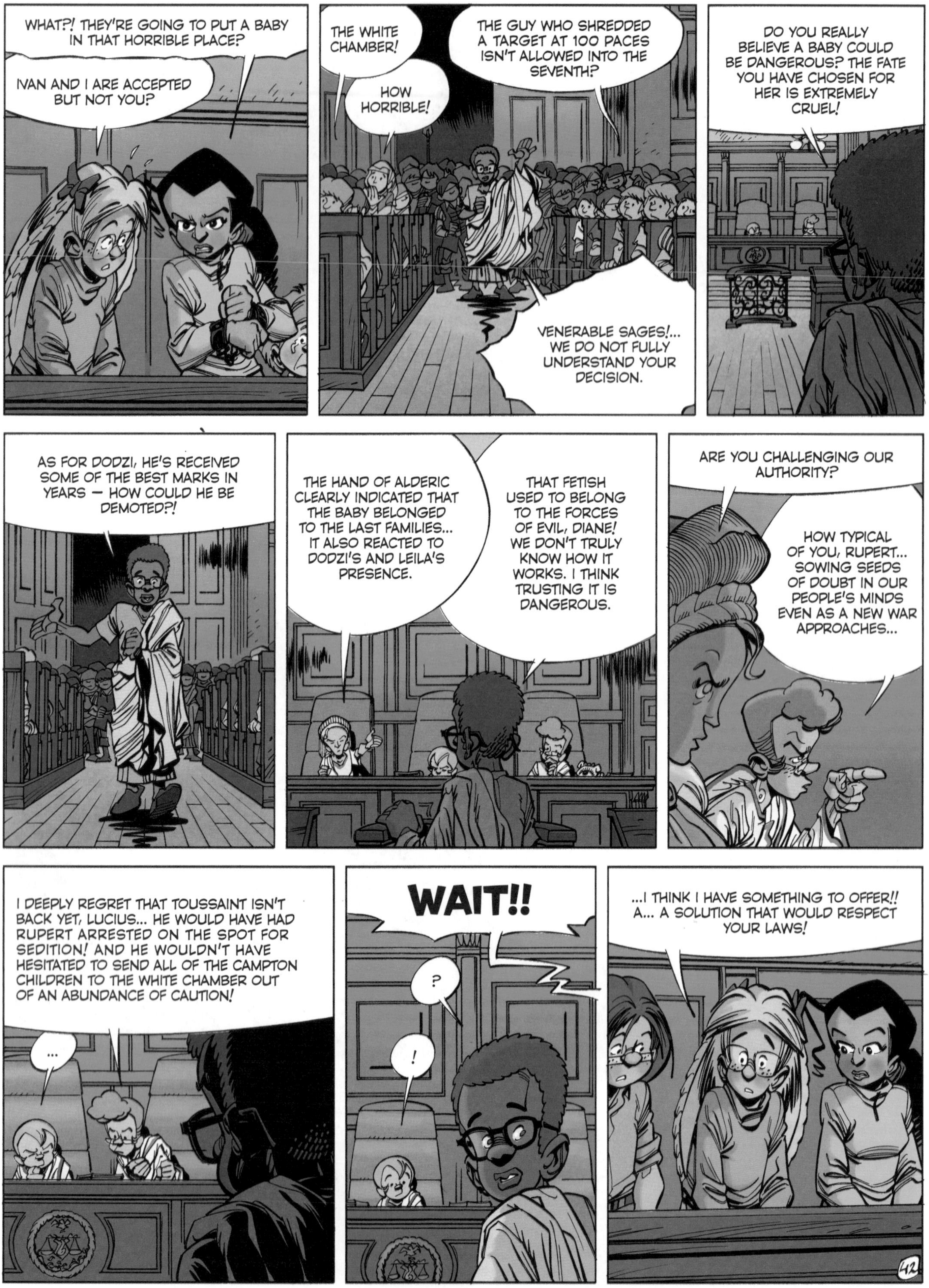

WHAT?! THEY'RE GOING TO PUT A BABY IN THAT HORRIBLE PLACE?
IVAN AND I ARE ACCEPTED BUT NOT YOU?
THE WHITE CHAMBER!
HOW HORRIBLE!
THE GUY WHO SHREDDED A TARGET AT 100 PACES ISN'T ALLOWED INTO THE SEVENTH?
VENERABLE SAGES!... WE DO NOT FULLY UNDERSTAND YOUR DECISION.
DO YOU REALLY BELIEVE A BABY COULD BE DANGEROUS? THE FATE YOU HAVE CHOSEN FOR HER IS EXTREMELY CRUEL!
AS FOR DODZI, HE'S RECEIVED SOME OF THE BEST MARKS IN YEARS — HOW COULD HE BE DEMOTED?!
THE HAND OF ALDERIC CLEARLY INDICATED THAT THE BABY BELONGED TO THE LAST FAMILIES... IT ALSO REACTED TO DODZI'S AND LEILA'S PRESENCE.
THAT FETISH USED TO BELONG TO THE FORCES OF EVIL, DIANE! WE DON'T TRULY KNOW HOW IT WORKS. I THINK TRUSTING IT IS DANGEROUS.
ARE YOU CHALLENGING OUR AUTHORITY?
HOW TYPICAL OF YOU, RUPERT... SOWING SEEDS OF DOUBT IN OUR PEOPLE'S MINDS EVEN AS A NEW WAR APPROACHES...
I DEEPLY REGRET THAT TOUSSAINT ISN'T BACK YET, LUCIUS... HE WOULD HAVE HAD RUPERT ARRESTED ON THE SPOT FOR SEDITION! AND HE WOULDN'T HAVE HESITATED TO SEND ALL OF THE CAMPTON CHILDREN TO THE WHITE CHAMBER OUT OF AN ABUNDANCE OF CAUTION!
...
WAIT!!
?
!
...I THINK I HAVE SOMETHING TO OFFER!! A... A SOLUTION THAT WOULD RESPECT YOUR LAWS!
42

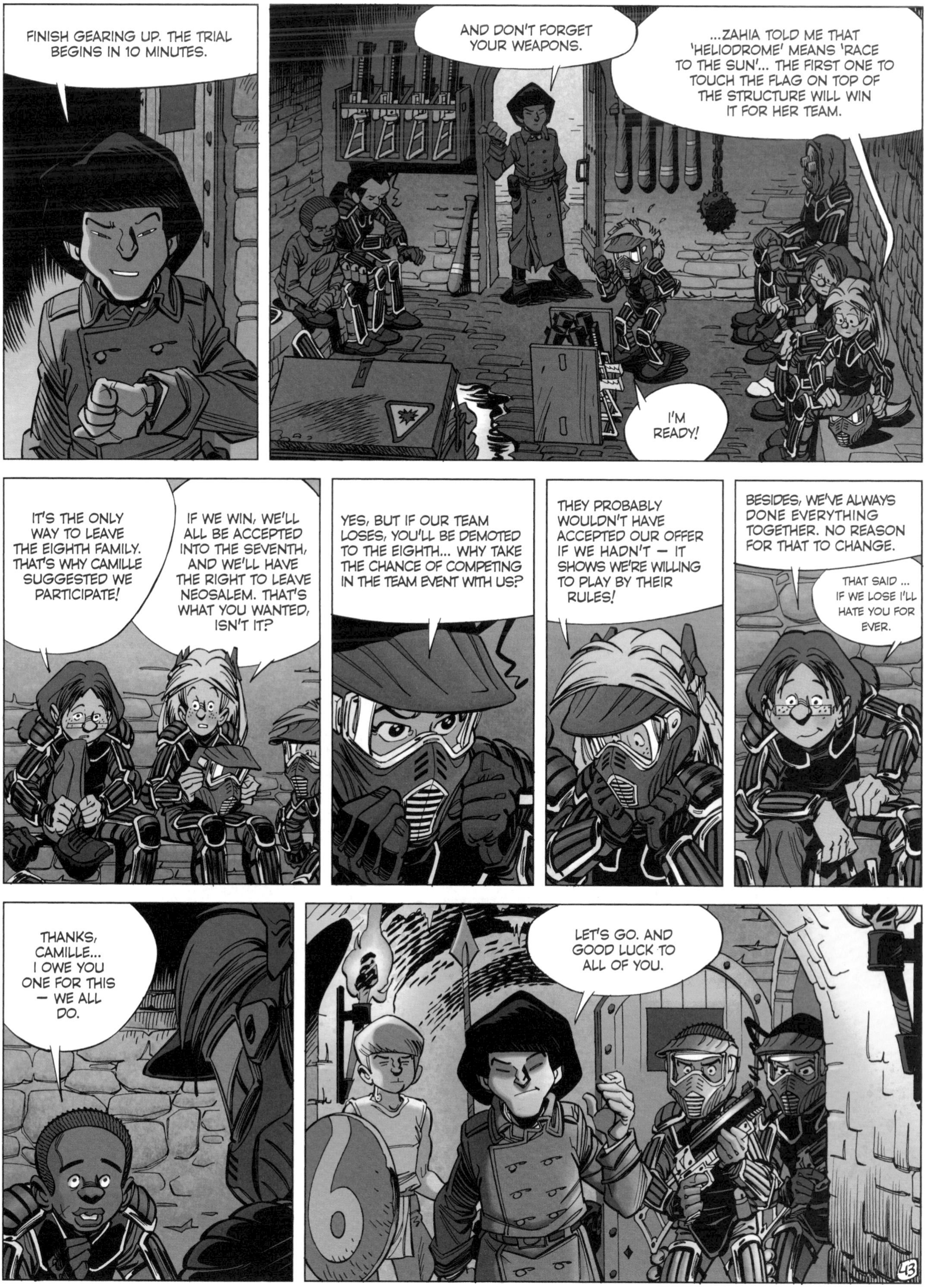

FINISH GEARING UP. THE TRIAL BEGINS IN 10 MINUTES.
AND DON'T FORGET YOUR WEAPONS.
...ZAHIA TOLD ME THAT 'HELIODROME' MEANS 'RACE TO THE SUN'... THE FIRST ONE TO TOUCH THE FLAG ON TOP OF THE STRUCTURE WILL WIN IT FOR HER TEAM.
I'M READY!
IT'S THE ONLY WAY TO LEAVE THE EIGHTH FAMILY. THAT'S WHY CAMILLE SUGGESTED WE PARTICIPATE!
IF WE WIN, WE'LL ALL BE ACCEPTED INTO THE SEVENTH, AND WE'LL HAVE THE RIGHT TO LEAVE NEOSALEM. THAT'S WHAT YOU WANTED, ISN'T IT?
YES, BUT IF OUR TEAM LOSES, YOU'LL BE DEMOTED TO THE EIGHTH... WHY TAKE THE CHANCE OF COMPETING IN THE TEAM EVENT WITH US?
THEY PROBABLY WOULDN'T HAVE ACCEPTED OUR OFFER IF WE HADN'T — IT SHOWS WE'RE WILLING TO PLAY BY THEIR RULES!
BESIDES, WE'VE ALWAYS DONE EVERYTHING TOGETHER. NO REASON FOR THAT TO CHANGE.
THAT SAID ... IF WE LOSE I'LL HATE YOU FOR EVER.
THANKS, CAMILLE... I OWE YOU ONE FOR THIS — WE ALL DO.
LET'S GO. AND GOOD LUCK TO ALL OF YOU.
6
43

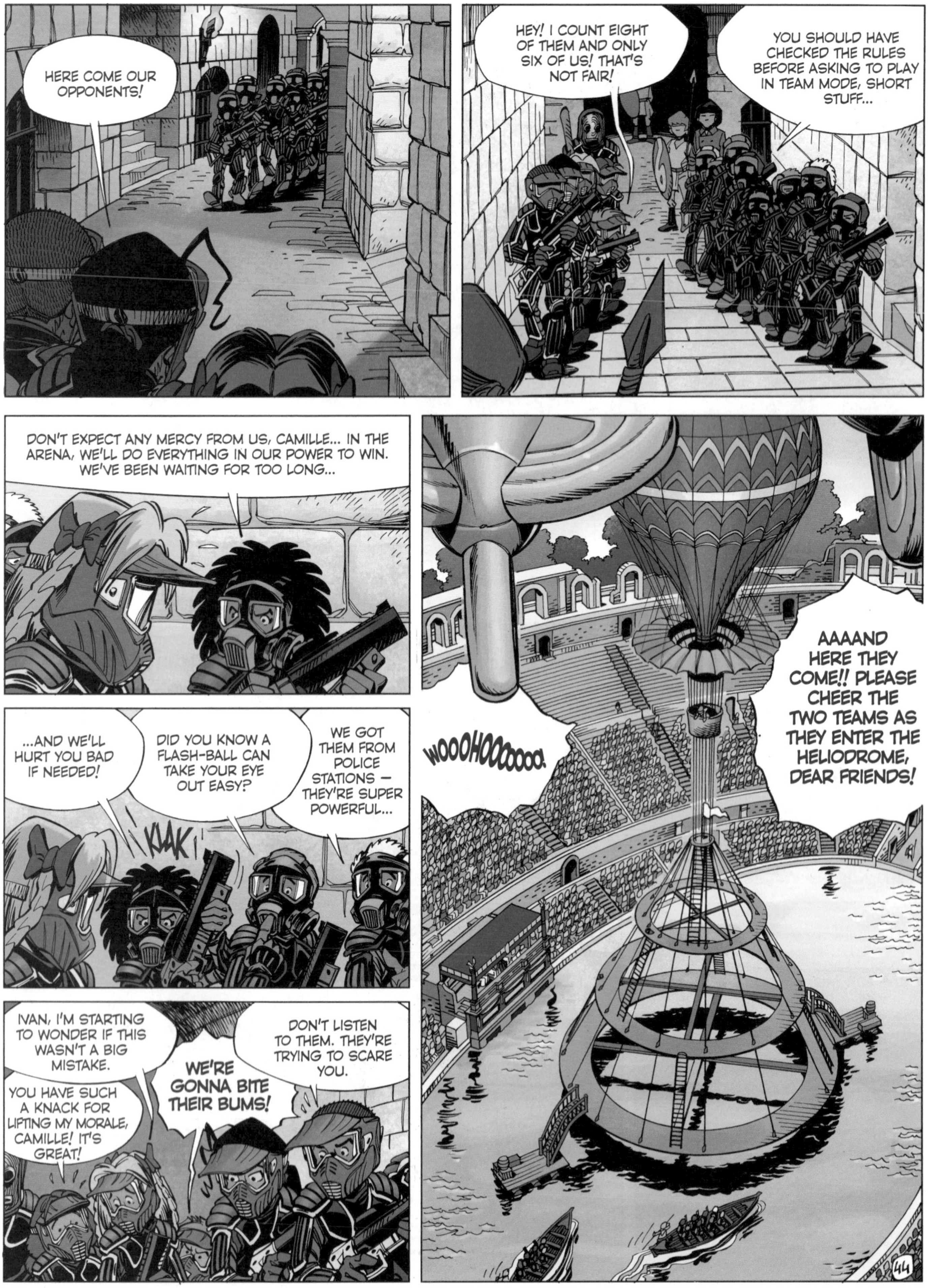
HERE COME OUR OPPONENTS!
HEY! I COUNT EIGHT OF THEM AND ONLY SIX OF US! THAT'S NOT FAIR!
YOU SHOULD HAVE CHECKED THE RULES BEFORE ASKING TO PLAY IN TEAM MODE, SHORT STUFF...
DON'T EXPECT ANY MERCY FROM US, CAMILLE... IN THE ARENA, WE'LL DO EVERYTHING IN OUR POWER TO WIN. WE'VE BEEN WAITING FOR TOO LONG...
...AND WE'LL HURT YOU BAD IF NEEDED!
DID YOU KNOW A FLASH-BALL CAN TAKE YOUR EYE OUT EASY?
WE GOT THEM FROM POLICE STATIONS — THEY'RE SUPER POWERFUL...
KLAK
IVAN, I'M STARTING TO WONDER IF THIS WASN'T A BIG MISTAKE.
YOU HAVE SUCH A KNACK FOR LIFTING MY MORALE, CAMILLE! IT'S GREAT!
WE'RE GONNA BITE THEIR BUMS!
DON'T LISTEN TO THEM. THEY'RE TRYING TO SCARE YOU.
WOOOHOOOOOOO!
AAAAND HERE THEY COME!! PLEASE CHEER THE TWO TEAMS AS THEY ENTER THE HELIODROME, DEAR FRIENDS!
44

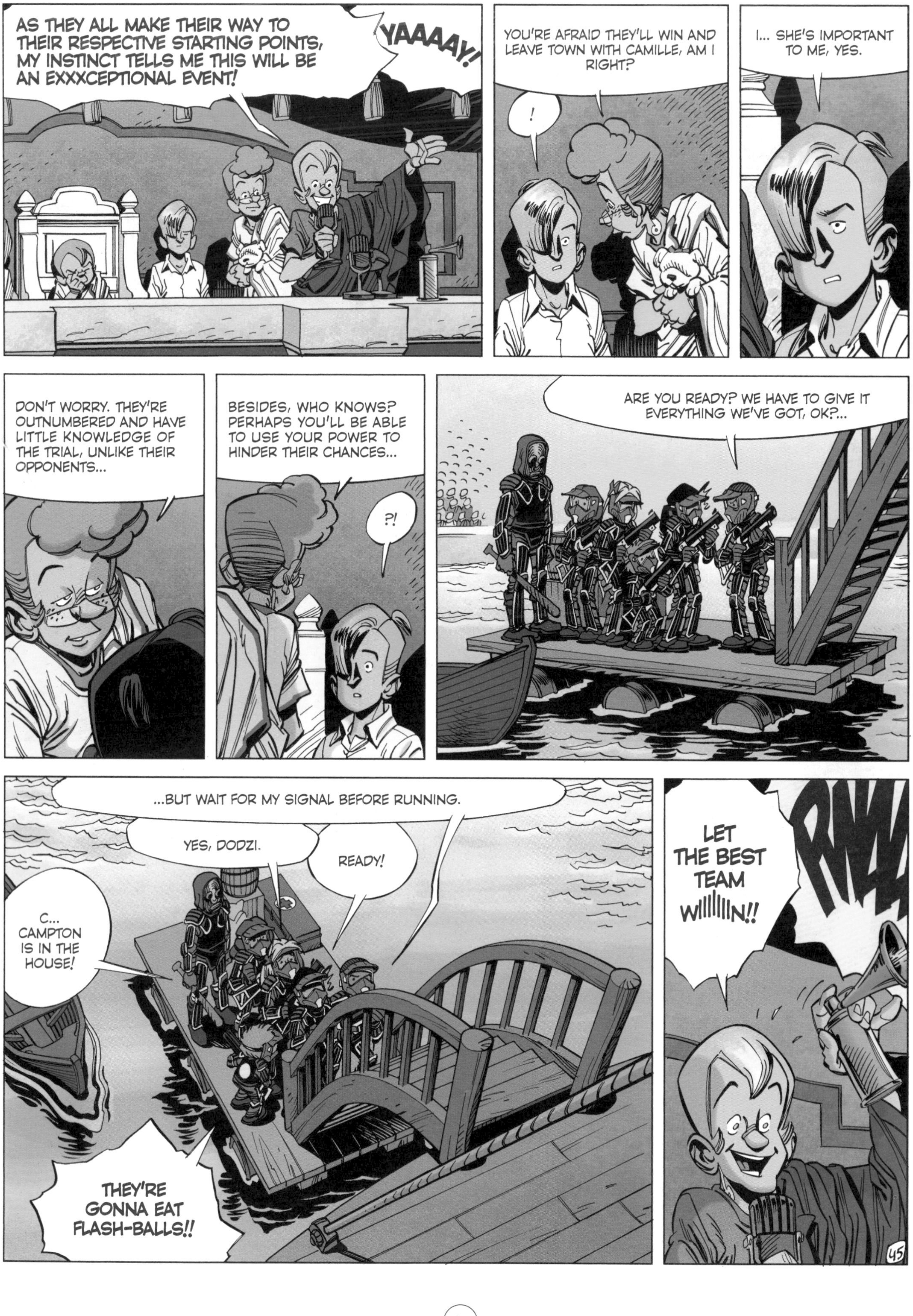
AS THEY ALL MAKE THEIR WAY TO THEIR RESPECTIVE STARTING POINTS, MY INSTINCT TELLS ME THIS WILL BE AN EXXXCEPTIONAL EVENT!
YAAAAY!
YOU'RE AFRAID THEY'LL WIN AND LEAVE TOWN WITH CAMILLE, AM I RIGHT?
!
I... SHE'S IMPORTANT TO ME, YES.
DON'T WORRY. THEY'RE OUTNUMBERED AND HAVE LITTLE KNOWLEDGE OF THE TRIAL, UNLIKE THEIR OPPONENTS...
BESIDES, WHO KNOWS? PERHAPS YOU'LL BE ABLE TO USE YOUR POWER TO HINDER THEIR CHANCES...
?!
ARE YOU READY? WE HAVE TO GIVE IT EVERYTHING WE'VE GOT, OK?...
...BUT WAIT FOR MY SIGNAL BEFORE RUNNING.
YES, DODZI.
READY!
C... CAMPTON IS IN THE HOUSE!
THEY'RE GONNA EAT FLASH-BALLS!!
LET THE BEST TEAM WIIIIIIN!!
45

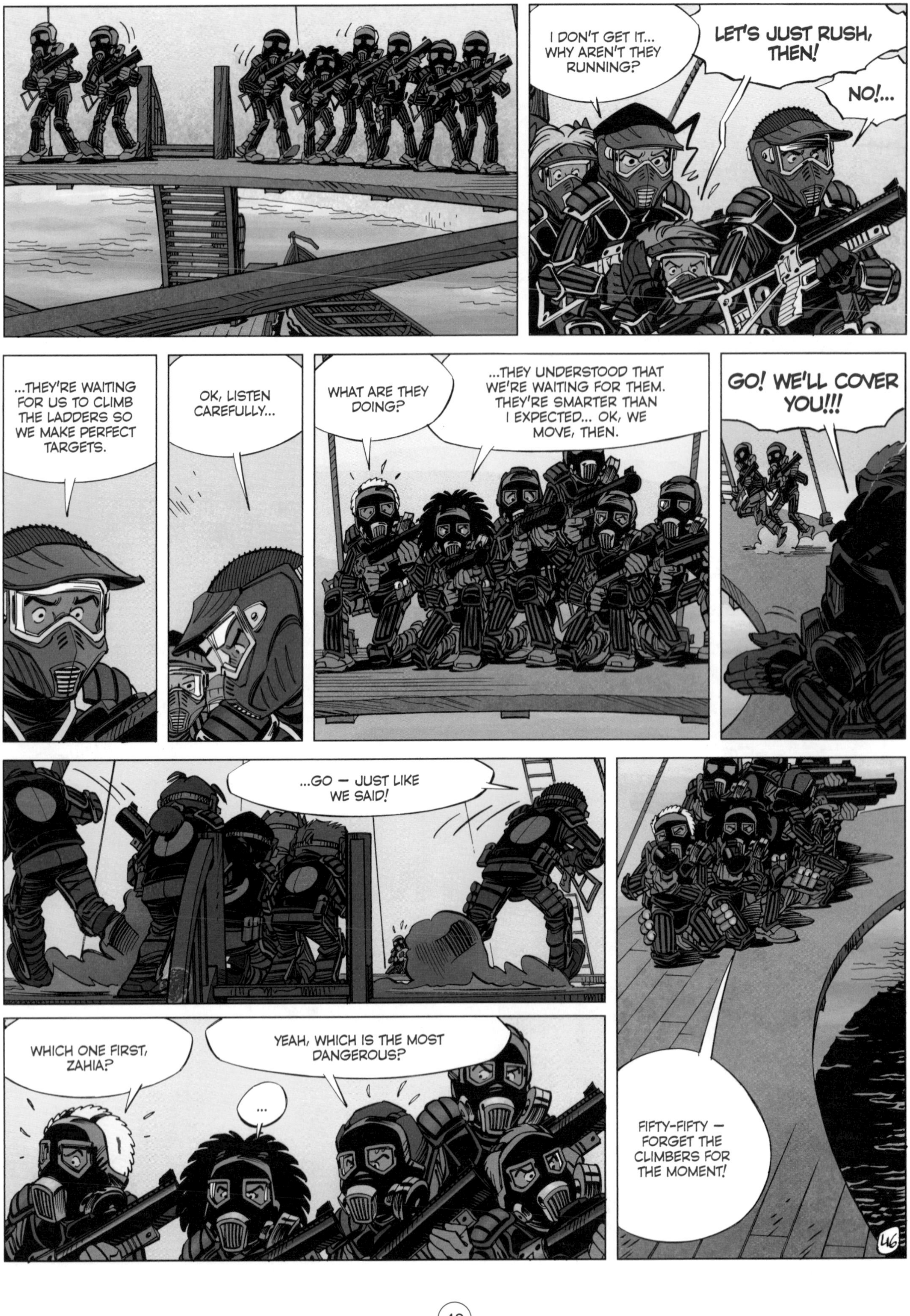

I DON'T GET IT... WHY AREN'T THEY RUNNING?
LET'S JUST RUSH, THEN!
NO!...
...THEY'RE WAITING FOR US TO CLIMB THE LADDERS SO WE MAKE PERFECT TARGETS.
OK, LISTEN CAREFULLY...
WHAT ARE THEY DOING?
...THEY UNDERSTOOD THAT WE'RE WAITING FOR THEM. THEY'RE SMARTER THAN I EXPECTED... OK, WE MOVE, THEN.
GO! WE'LL COVER YOU!!!
...GO — JUST LIKE WE SAID!
WHICH ONE FIRST, ZAHIA?
...
YEAH, WHICH IS THE MOST DANGEROUS?
FIFTY-FIFTY — FORGET THE CLIMBERS FOR THE MOMENT!
46

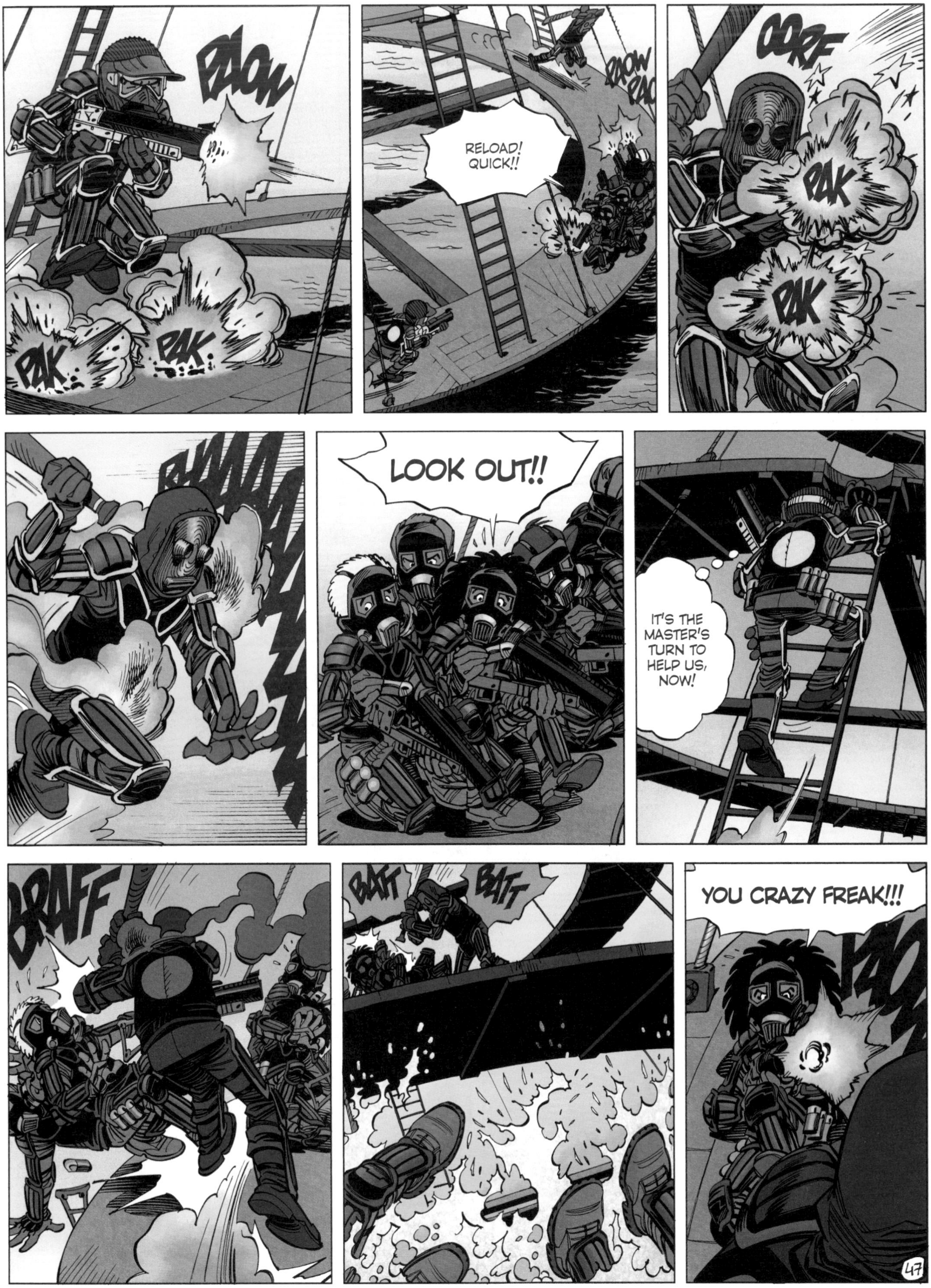
BLAOW
PAK
PAK
RELOAD! QUICK!!
OORF
PAK
PAK
LOOK OUT!!
IT'S THE MASTER'S TURN TO HELP US, NOW!
BRAFF
BATT
BATT
YOU CRAZY FREAK!!!
47

HA! HA!

WHOA!! THE MASTER OF KNIVES GOT THREE ALL BY HIMSELF!

THAT STILL LEAVES FIVE OF THEM, REMEMBER!

TAKE COVER — THE OTHERS ARE GOING TO...

AAH!

...LIGHT US UP!

URFFF!

?!

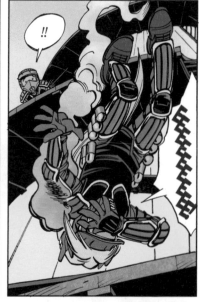

!!

SPLOOOSH!

HHHHH!!

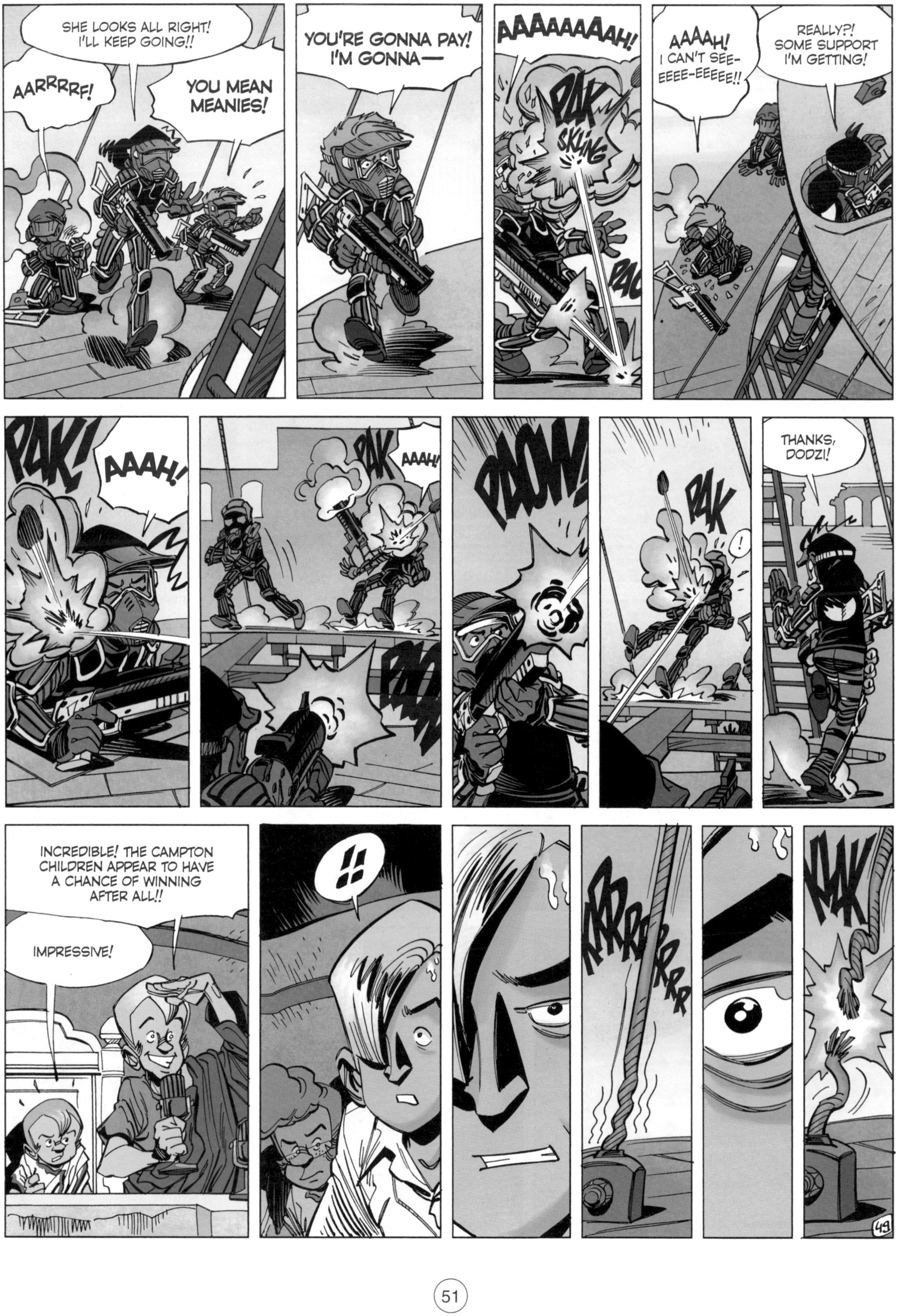
SHE LOOKS ALL RIGHT! I'LL KEEP GOING!!
AARRRRF!
YOU MEAN MEANIES!
YOU'RE GONNA PAY! I'M GONNA—
AAAAAAAAH!
PAK
SKLING
PAC
AAAAH! I CAN'T SEE-EEEE-EEEEE!!
REALLY?! SOME SUPPORT I'M GETTING!
PAK!
AAAH!
PAK
AAAH!
PLOM!
PAK
!
THANKS, DODZI!
INCREDIBLE! THE CAMPTON CHILDREN APPEAR TO HAVE A CHANCE OF WINNING AFTER ALL!!
IMPRESSIVE!
!!
KRRRRRRRRR
KLAK
49

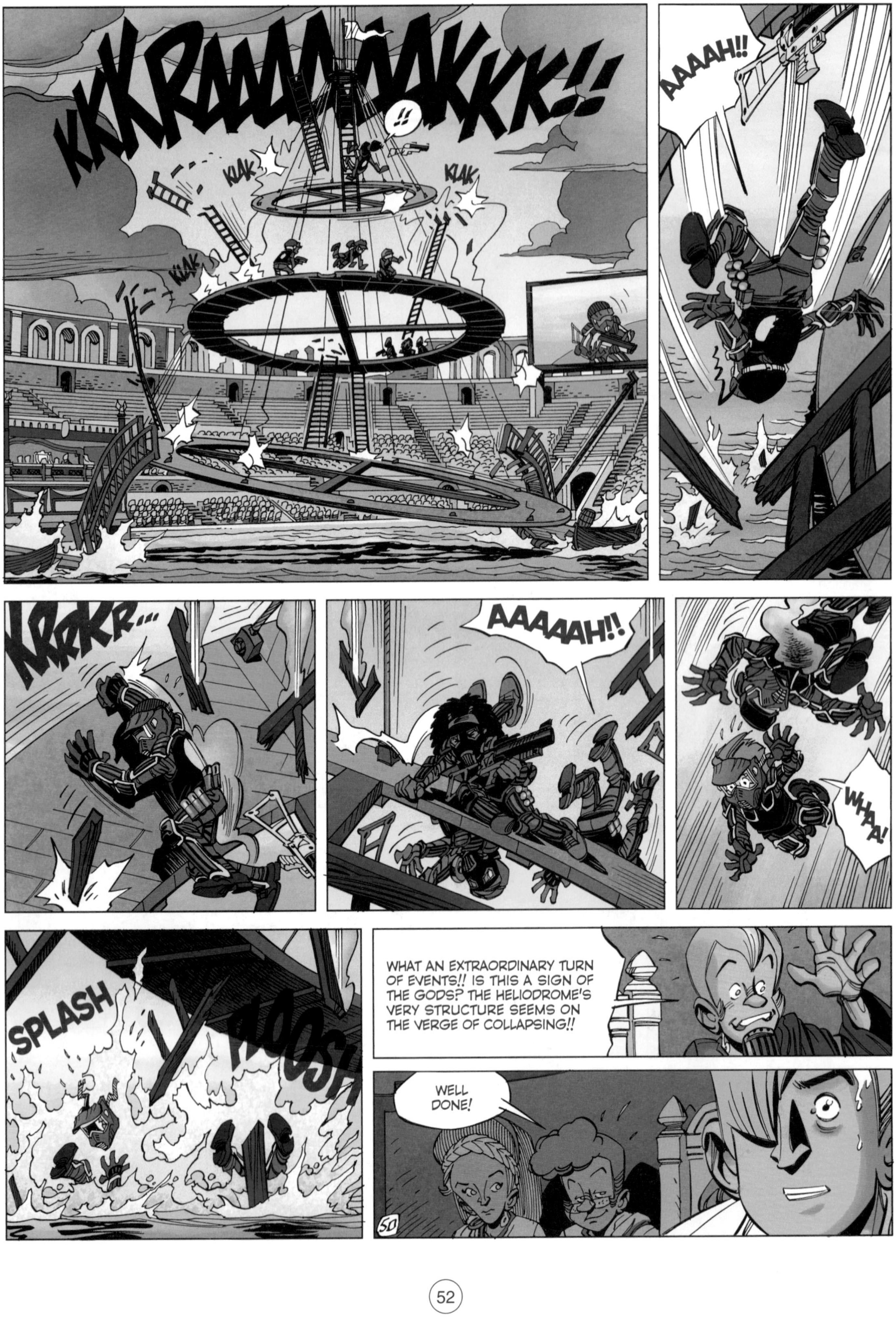
KKKRAAAAAAKKKK!!
!!
KLAK
KLAK
KLAK
AAAAH!!
KRRKR...
AAAAAH!!
WHAA!
SPLASH
WHAT AN EXTRAORDINARY TURN OF EVENTS!! IS THIS A SIGN OF THE GODS? THE HELIODROME'S VERY STRUCTURE SEEMS ON THE VERGE OF COLLAPSING!!
WELL DONE!

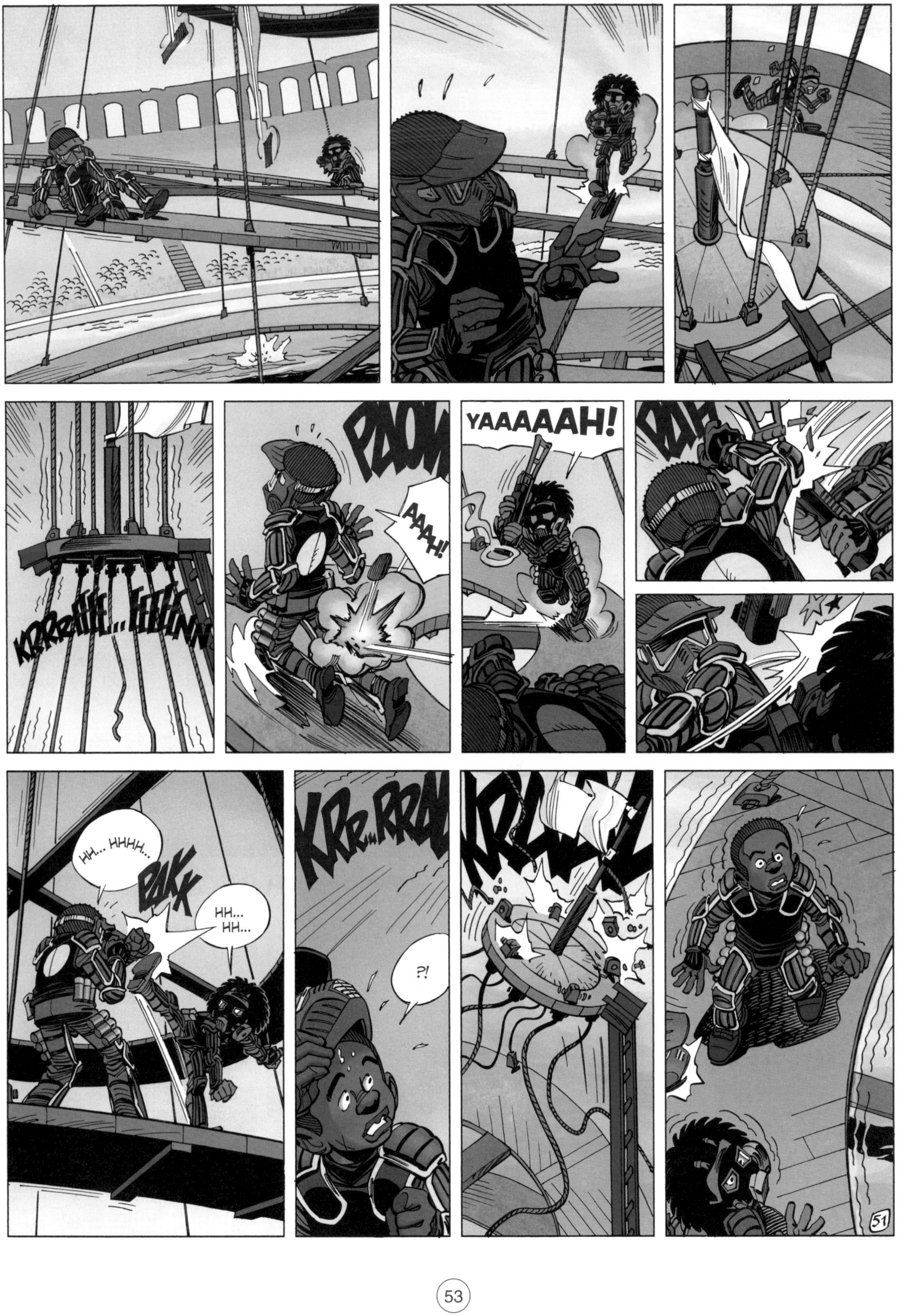

AAAAH!
YAAAAAH!
HH... HHHH...
PAKK
HH...
HH...
?!
51

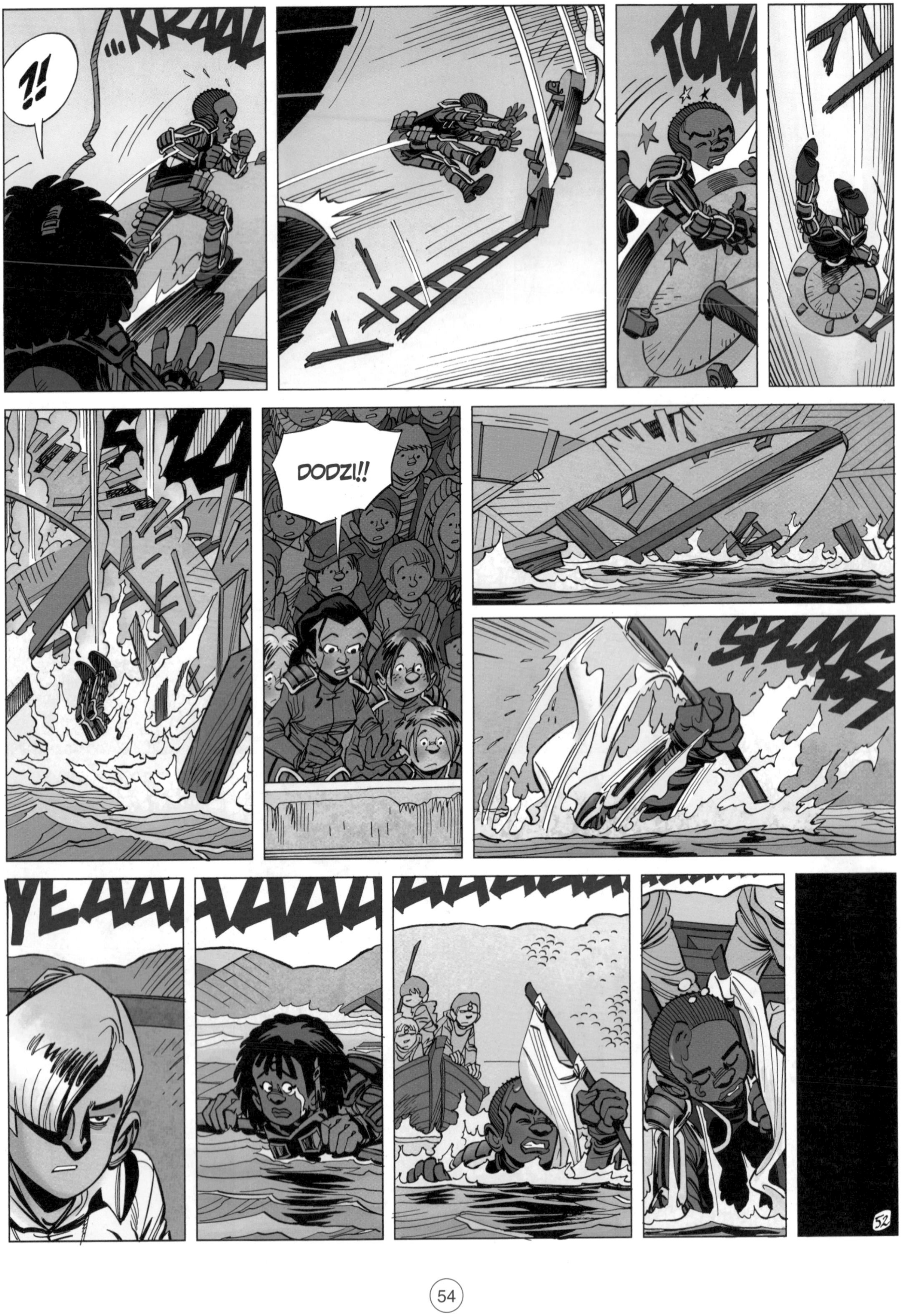
?!
DODZI!!

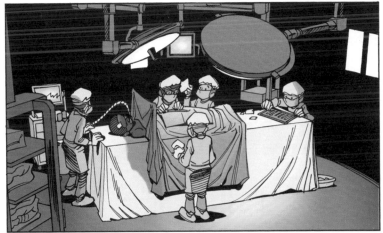

HOW ARE YOU FEELING?

BETTER... THANKS FOR COMING TO SEE ME SO SOON.

YOU SCARED US BAD!

WHAT ABOUT THE MASTER OF KNIVES? WHERE IS HE?

THEY WON'T LET HIM OUT OF HIS CELL UNTIL HE LEAVES TOWN WITH US.

I'M AFRAID THEY WOULDN'T BUDGE ABOUT LUCIE, THOUGH. WE INSISTED, BUT SHE'LL REMAIN IN THE WHITE CHAMBER.

CAN YOU BELIEVE A BABY IS THE CHAMPION OF EVIL?

...I CAN'T WAIT UNTIL WE LEAVE THOSE 'FIRST FAMILIES' AND THEIR DUMB LAWS!

YEAH, BUT TO GO WHERE?

...I NEED TO GO BACK TO THE MOUNTAINS WE CROSSED ON OUR WAY HERE.

HUH? WHAT FOR?

SOMETHING I NEED TO CHECK ... BUT I DON'T WANT TO FORCE ANYONE TO COME ALONG.

HEY! WE SAID WE'RE STAYING TOGETHER!

UH... THAT WAS TRUE FOR THE TRIAL, BUT...

...I... I'VE DECIDED TO STAY HERE ... WITH SAUL.

!

?!

?!

?

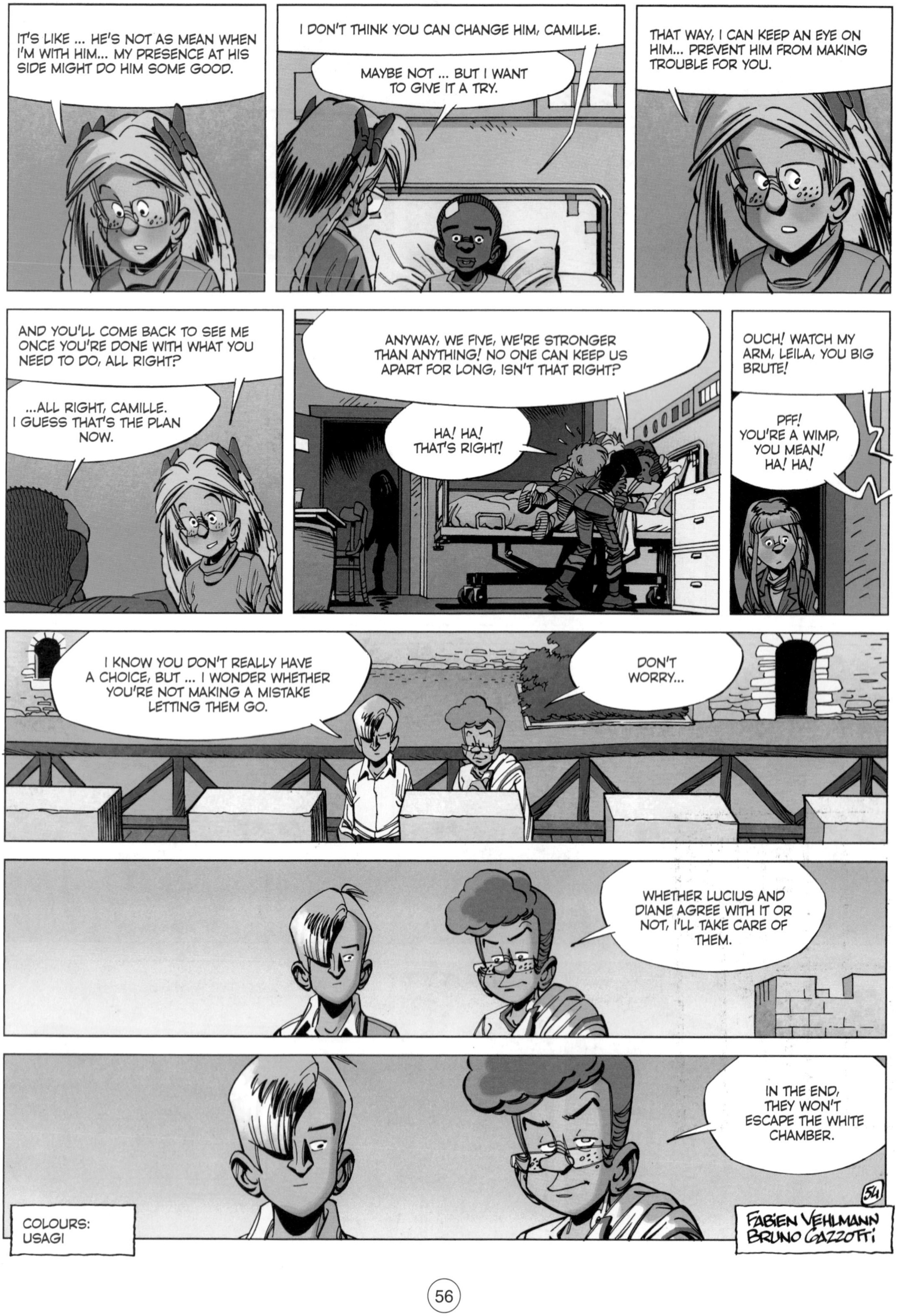
IT'S LIKE ... HE'S NOT AS MEAN WHEN I'M WITH HIM... MY PRESENCE AT HIS SIDE MIGHT DO HIM SOME GOOD.
I DON'T THINK YOU CAN CHANGE HIM, CAMILLE.
MAYBE NOT ... BUT I WANT TO GIVE IT A TRY.
THAT WAY, I CAN KEEP AN EYE ON HIM... PREVENT HIM FROM MAKING TROUBLE FOR YOU.
AND YOU'LL COME BACK TO SEE ME ONCE YOU'RE DONE WITH WHAT YOU NEED TO DO, ALL RIGHT?
...ALL RIGHT, CAMILLE. I GUESS THAT'S THE PLAN NOW.
ANYWAY, WE FIVE, WE'RE STRONGER THAN ANYTHING! NO ONE CAN KEEP US APART FOR LONG, ISN'T THAT RIGHT?
HA! HA! THAT'S RIGHT!
OUCH! WATCH MY ARM, LEILA, YOU BIG BRUTE!
PFF! YOU'RE A WIMP, YOU MEAN! HA! HA!
I KNOW YOU DON'T REALLY HAVE A CHOICE, BUT ... I WONDER WHETHER YOU'RE NOT MAKING A MISTAKE LETTING THEM GO.
DON'T WORRY...
WHETHER LUCIUS AND DIANE AGREE WITH IT OR NOT, I'LL TAKE CARE OF THEM.
IN THE END, THEY WON'T ESCAPE THE WHITE CHAMBER.
54
COLOURS: USAGI
FABIEN VEHLMANN
BRUNO GAZZOTTI